D1511891

Public Library
y St.

West Branch, IA 52358

DISCOVERING CAREERS FOR YOUR FUTURE

law enforcement

Ferguson
An imprint of Infobase Publishing

Discovering Careers for Your Future: Law Enforcement

Copyright © 2008 by Infobase Publishing

Ferguson
An imprint of Infobase Publishing
132 West 31st Street
New York NY 10001

Library of Congress Cataloging-in-Publication Data

Discovering careers for your future : law enforcement.
    p. cm.
    Includes bibliographical references and index.
    ISBN-13: 978-0-8160-7293-4 (acid-free paper)
    ISBN-10: 0-8160-7293-0 (acid-free paper) 1. Law enforcement—Vocational guidance—United States—Juvenile literature. I. Ferguson Publishing.
    HV9950.D597 2008
    363.2023'73—dc22
                                          2007050864

Ferguson books are available at special discounts when purchased in bulk quantities for businesses, associations, institutions, or sales promotions. Please call our Special Sales Department in New York at (212) 967-8800 or (800) 322-8755.

You can find Ferguson on the World Wide Web at http://www.fergpubco.com

Text design by Mary Susan Ryan-Flynn
Cover design by Jooyoung An

Printed in the United States of America

EB MSRF 10 9 8 7 6 5 4 3 2 1

This book is printed on acid-free paper.

Contents

Introduction I

Airport Security Workers 5

Border Patrol Agents 9

Bounty Hunters 13

Corrections Officers 17

Crime Analysts 20

Customs Officials 24

Deputy U.S. Marshals 28

Detectives 32

FBI Agents 36

Fire Inspectors and Investigators 40

Firefighters 44

Forensic Experts 48

Health and Regulatory Inspectors 52

Park Rangers 56

Parole Officers 61

Police Officers 64

Polygraph Examiners 68

Process Servers 72

Secret Service Special Agents 76

Security Consultants and Guards 80

Glossary 84

Index of Job Titles 88

Browse and Learn More 90

Introduction

You may not have decided yet what you want to be in the future. And you don't have to decide right away. You do know that right now you are interested in law enforcement. Do any of the statements below describe you? If so, you may want to begin thinking about what a career in some area of law enforcement might mean for you.

___I can think on my feet and react quickly.
___Physical education is my favorite subject in school.
___I have leadership abilities.
___I enjoy learning about government and the law.
___I like to solve puzzles.
___I like all kinds of physical activity.
___I always try to obey the law.
___I like television shows and movies about police officers and firefighters.
___I like to read detective stories and spy stories.
___I am curious and ask a lot of questions.
___I am good at handling stressful situations.
___I enjoy working as a hall monitor at school.
___I am not easily frightened.
___I like to help others.

Discovering Careers for Your Future: Law Enforcement is a book about careers in law enforcement, from airport security workers to security consultants and guards. People who pursue careers in law enforcement are interested in helping and protecting others and enforcing the laws of our country. Their work usually requires physical activity and some degree of danger. Most people who work in law enforcement consider work in the field to be a "calling," and despite the potential danger, get a lot of personal satisfaction from keeping people safe.

This book describes many possibilities for future careers in law enforcement. Read through it and see how the different careers are connected. For example, if you are interested in police and protective services work, you will want to read the chapters on airport security workers, border patrol agents, customs officials, deputy U.S. marshals, FBI agents, police officers, and Secret Service special agents. If danger intrigues you, read the chapters on bounty hunters and firefighters. If you want to investigate crimes and try to prevent them from happening, you will want to read the chapters on crime analysts, detectives, fire inspectors and investigators, and forensic experts. Other options in the field include corrections officers, health and regulatory inspectors, parole officers, polygraph examiners, and process servers. Go ahead and explore!

What Do They Do?

The first section of each chapter begins with a heading such as "What FBI Agents Do" or "What Park Rangers Do." It tells what it's like to work at this job. It describes typical responsibilities and assignments. You will find out about working conditions. Which careers involve desk work? Which ones involve working outdoors in all kinds of weather? Which careers involve a lot of danger? What tools and equipment are used? This section answers all these questions.

How Do I Prepare for a Career in Law Enforcement?

The section called "Education and Training" tells you what schooling you need for employment in each job—a high school diploma, training at a junior college, a college degree, or more. It also talks about on-the-job training that you could expect to receive after you're hired, and whether or not you must complete an apprenticeship program.

How Much Do People in Law Enforcement Careers Earn?

The Earnings section gives the average salary figures for the job described in the chapter. These figures provide you with a general idea of how much money people with this job can make. Keep in mind that many people really earn more or less than the amounts given here because actual salaries depend on many factors, such as the size of the company, its location, and the amount of education, training, and experience you have. Generally, but not always, bigger companies located in major cities pay more than smaller ones in smaller cities and towns, and people with more education, training, and experience earn more. Also remember that these figures are current averages. They will probably be different by the time you are ready to enter the workforce.

What Will the Future Be Like for Careers in Law Enforcement?

The Outlook section discusses the employment outlook for each career: whether the total number of people employed in this career will increase or decrease in the coming years and whether jobs in this field will be easy or hard to find. These predictions are based on economic conditions, the size and makeup of the population, foreign competition, and new technology. Phrases such as "faster than the average," "about as fast as the average," and "slower than the average" are used by the U.S. Department of Labor to describe job growth predicted by government data.

Keep in mind that these predictions are general statements. No one knows for sure what the future will be like. And remember that the employment outlook is a general statement about an industry and does not necessarily apply to everyone. A determined and talented person may be able to find a job in an industry or career with the worst kind of outlook. And a person without ambition and the proper training will find it difficult to find a job in even a booming industry or career field.

Where Can I Find More Information?

Each chapter includes a sidebar called "For More Info." It lists organizations that you can contact to find out more about the field and careers in the field. You will find names, addresses, phone numbers, e-mail addresses, and Web sites.

Extras

Every chapter has a few extras. There are photos that show workers in action. There are sidebars and notes on ways to explore the field, fun facts, highlights of recommended qualities, or lists of resources that might be helpful. At the end of the book you will find three additional sections: Glossary, Index of Job Titles, and Browse and Learn More. The Glossary gives brief definitions of words that relate to education, career training, or employment with which you may be unfamiliar. The Index of Job Titles includes all the job titles mentioned in the book. The Browse and Learn More section lists law enforcement books and Web sites to explore.

It's not too soon to think about your future. We hope you discover several possible career choices. Happy hunting!

Airport Security Workers

What Airport Security Workers Do

Airport security workers help keep passengers and airport workers safe in our nation's airports and aircraft. Three of the most important professions in the field are *security screeners, air marshals,* and *security directors.*

The most visible airport security worker is the security screener. These workers are also called *baggage and passenger screeners.* They use computers, X-ray machines, and handheld scanners to screen bags and their owners passing through airport terminals. In addition to using technology to help them identify dangerous items, they also have to depend on their own eyesight to catch suspicious behavior for signs of danger.

Air marshals, also called *security agents,* have the demanding job of protecting airline passengers and staff from on-board threats, such as terrorists, hijackers, bombs, or other weapons. These workers are often covert in their operations, meaning they may be dressed and seated like an average passenger to be able to watch for suspicious behavior and to surprise a potential attacker. Many of the details of air marshal jobs, such as their exact number and identities, routes, and training procedures, are classified to protect national security. However the basics of their job is much like a Secret Service special agent. They must be attentive to all activity that goes on around them,

Did You Know?

○ The average air marshal flies 181 days per year.
○ Air marshals fly about 15 days per month.
○ Most air marshals spend approximately 900 hours in an aircraft per year.
○ Air marshals spend five hours in an aircraft each day they are on duty.

Source: Transportation Security Administration

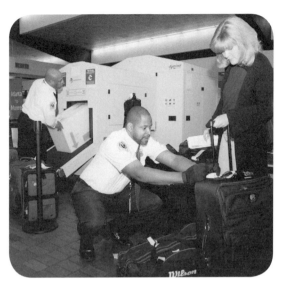

A federal security screener prepares a traveler's bags for screening. (Gregory Smith, Associated Press)

identify potential threats to security, and deal with dangerous individuals or objects once exposed on board. The main difference between air marshals and other security agents is that they must be trained and able to handle possible warfare in a confined space at 30,000 or more feet in the air.

Another important airport security job is that of security director. These workers manage all security personnel within an airport. They oversee the hiring, training, and work of baggage and passenger screeners, air marshals, and other security guards. In the nation's largest airports, such as LaGuardia in New York City or O'Hare in Chicago, directors are in charge of hundreds of workers. Because of the high level of responsibility held by these workers, security directors often have previous experience in crisis management or law enforcement, having

To Be a Successful Security Screener, You Should . . .

- ○ have good vision and hearing
- ○ be focused and alert
- ○ be personable and courteous to people being screened who may be impatient or rude
- ○ be able to manage crowds
- ○ be able to maintain your composure in stressful conditions
- ○ have excellent communication skills
- ○ be able to work as a member of a team

worked in positions such as police chiefs or military officers.

Education and Training

In high school, take classes in history and government to familiarize yourself with previous events that have threatened our national security, such as hijackings and terrorist operations. Math classes can be beneficial because as a security worker, you must be analytical and observant to identify and catch dangers before they happen.

All airport security workers, from screeners to directors, are highly trained before starting their jobs. Screeners are trained on how to operate and identify dangerous objects from X-ray machines to handheld wands. They also must be ready to deal with potentially dangerous individuals. Screeners currently receive 40 hours of training before their first day at work, and receive an additional 60 hours of training while on the job. This training period may be extended due to increased scrutiny on screeners' performance and the perception of heightened national security risks.

Air marshals are highly trained before starting their jobs. They receive rigorous instruction in classified training centers across the country, and come to the job with previous on-the-job experience from serving in a military or civilian police force. Some of the topics

EXPLORING

○ Since air marshals work under cover, you won't be able to observe them at work. You can learn about other airport security workers by watching these people at work your next time at the airport. Notice how many people are involved in screening luggage and passengers. Although you should not talk to screeners and other security staff while they are working, you may be able to schedule an interview with security personnel while they are on break or perhaps over the phone or via e-mail. Ask your teacher or guidance counselor to help arrange an interview.

○ You can also learn about security jobs at your local library or online. Explore the Web sites of the Transportation Security Administration and the Federal Aviation Administration for facts and job descriptions, changes in policy, and even summer camp opportunities. The links at the end of this article are good places to start your research. (See "For More Info.")

FOR MORE INFO

The FAA offers a wealth of information on its Web site, from airline accident statistics to career guidance. Visit the Education & Research section for information on summer camps for middle and high school students interested in aviation careers.

Federal Aviation Administration (FAA)
800 Independence Avenue SW
Washington, DC 20591
Tel: 866-835-5322
http://www.faa.gov

According to its Web site, the TSA "sets the standard for excellence in transportation security through its people, processes, and technologies." Explore the site for details on the nation's threat advisory level and tips on flying and packing safely.

Transportation Security Administration (TSA)
TSA-21 Human Capital
601 South 12th Street
Arlington, VA 22202-4220
http://www.tsa.gov

in which they receive training include criminal terrorist behavior recognition, investigative techniques, firearms proficiency, aircraft specific tactics, and self-defense measures in close quarters.

Security directors must have previous federal security experience and are trained for up to 400 hours before taking on the responsibility of directing an entire airport security staff.

Earnings

Most full-time screeners earn salaries of $23,000 to $35,000 or more a year. Their pay increases as their level of experience and responsibility increases. Salaries for air marshals range from approximately $35,000 for new workers to $80,000 or more for the most experienced workers. Security directors earn salaries that range from $79,000 to $123,000 or more. Directors who work at large airports can earn salaries of $150,000 or more.

Outlook

With the new awareness of airline dangers following the 2001 terrorist attacks, the public will continue to rely on airport security workers to protect people from terrorists and other dangers. There will always be a critical need for qualified and skilled individuals to protect airports, airplanes, and passengers from security threats.

Border Patrol Agents

What Border Patrol Agents Do

In order to protect the people of the United States, the government has formed laws that specify which persons and which products can enter the country. However, many attempts are made to break these laws and cross the border illegally. *Border patrol agents* have a mission to prevent illegal entry into the United States at the borders and to deport or arrest people who attempt to enter illegally. They are employed by U.S. Customs and Border Protection (CBP), a branch of the U.S. Department of Homeland Security.

Border patrol agents are federal law enforcement agents, a group that also includes U.S. marshals and FBI agents. They all have a duty to enforce the laws of the U.S. government. Under U.S. law, people from other countries who wish to enter the country must apply to the government for this privilege. Depending on which country they are from, many of those who are visiting or wish to work or study in the United States must obtain visas. Those who wish to live here permanently must apply for residency status. Border patrol agents are on guard to make sure that people follow these rules.

Along the U.S. borders with Mexico and Canada, border patrol agents work 24 hours a day. They use many different tactics to catch people sneaking over the border. They patrol the border in jeeps

Did You Know?

○ The border patrol was founded in 1924.

○ Border patrol agents are responsible for patrolling more than 6,900 miles of Canadian and Mexican international land borders and more than 2,000 miles of coastal waters surrounding the Florida peninsula and the island of Puerto Rico.

○ The border patrol has made more than 15.6 million apprehensions since 1994.

○ In 2005, border patrol agents seized more than 1.2 million pounds of marijuana and more than 12,300 pounds of cocaine. These illegal drugs had a street value of more than $1.4 billion.

EXPLORING

○ You will not be able to receive direct experience with border patrolling, but physical exercise and knowledge of geography will help you prepare for this career.

○ Visit the National Border Patrol Museum (http://www.borderpatrol museum.com) in El Paso, Texas, to learn more about the field.

○ Try to interview a border patrol agent about his or her career. Ask the following questions: What are your main and secondary job duties? What do you like least and most about your job? How did you train for this field? What advice would you give a young person who is interested in the field?

and, in more rugged terrain, on horseback. Border patrol agents routinely fly helicopters over areas where many people try to enter the country illegally. At night they scan the horizon with special night-vision goggles. They are also posted at regular border crossings to make sure that people are not hidden inside cars and trucks in order to enter the country illegally.

When people are caught trying to cross the border illegally, border patrol agents send them back across the border. Because of their duties, border patrol agents need to stay up to date on many laws and regulations, including those dealing with arrest, detention, and search and seizure.

In recent years, the prevention of drug smuggling has become a major part of the border patrol officer's job. Agents sometimes use drug-sniffing dogs to help find where drugs have been hidden. Following the September 2001 terrorist attacks, border patrol agents must pay careful attention to who is let into the United States.

Education and Training

To prepare for this career, you should take high school courses in geography, government, history, social studies, communications, political science, and Spanish. Thorough knowledge of Spanish will give you an advantage over other job applicants.

A high school diploma or its equivalent is required to become a border patrol agent, but a bachelor's degree is preferred. Those who are accepted into the border patrol agent-training program receive five months of training at the CBP Border Patrol Academy in Artesia, New Mexico.

In the training program, you will learn the laws you will need in the course of your duties. You will undergo physical training and learn the safe use of firearms. You must also study Spanish, a requirement unique to this branch of law enforcement. After graduation, all border patrol agents start out stationed along the Mexican border.

Earnings

Border patrol agents begin at the GS-5, GS-7, or GS-9 pay grade (a pay scale established by the federal government), depending on their level of education and experience. Salaries at the GS-5 level ranged from $25,623 to $33,309 in 2007; at the GS-7 level, $31,740 to $41,262; and at the GS-9 level, $38,824 to $50,470. The highest nonsupervisory grade for a border patrol officer is GS-11, which paid between $46,974 and $61,068 in 2007.

Outlook

Employment for all police officers and detectives (including border patrol agents) is projected to increase about as fast

To Be a Successful Border Patrol Agent, You Should . . .

- be decisive
- have integrity
- be attentive to detail
- be courteous and professional to those you apprehend
- be physically fit, including having good vision and hearing
- be able to speak Spanish
- be willing to work long hours
- be able to work in demanding weather conditions or tough terrain

Are You Up for the Job?

Working as a border patrol agent is demanding. You will be required to hike through deserts, canyons, and mountains as well as work in blistering heat, driving rain, high winds, and freezing temperatures and snowstorms. You might need to chase down an individual who is attempting to enter the United States illegally. You may even have to defend yourself against a drug smuggler or suspected terrorist. To ensure that it hires only top agents, U.S. Customs and Border Protection has established three preemployment fitness tests that help weed out unqualified applicants. These include a push-up test, sit-up test, and a cardiovascular endurance step test. Here are the requirements for each test. Are you up to the challenge?

Push-up Test
Applicants must complete 20 proper form push-ups in 60 seconds.

Sit-up Test
Applicants must complete 25 proper form sit-ups in 60 seconds.

Step Test
Applicants must step up and down on a 12-inch-high step at a rate of 30 steps per minute for a total of five minutes.

FOR MORE INFO

For career information, visit CBP's Web site
U.S. Customs and Border Protection (CBP)
U.S. Department of Homeland Security
1300 Pennsylvania Avenue NW
Washington, DC 20229
Tel: 202-354-1000
http://www.cbp.gov

as the average. There has been growing public support for drug prevention activities, including the prevention of drug smuggling. Public support for the war on drugs has enabled U.S. Customs and Border Protection to continue to increase its surveillance of U.S. borders. After the terrorist attacks in 2001, growing concerns over the level of illegal immigration have created an urgent need for more border patrol agents.

Bounty Hunters

What Bounty Hunters Do

When people are arrested, they can sometimes get out of jail if they guarantee they will appear in court on a certain date and post a large amount of money, called bail. Most people who are arrested don't have money to pay for bail, so a bail bondsman provides the money to the court. (The person pays the bondsman a fee—usually 10 percent of the actual posted bond.) If the person does not show up on the court date, the bondsman usually hires a *bounty hunter* to track down the fugitive and return him or her to the police or other law enforcement agency. The bounty hunter is paid only if the fugitive is returned to court.

The goal of the bounty hunter is to locate the fugitive as safely and quickly as possible. To do this, they must have good research, detection, and law enforcement skills. They interview family, friends, and coworkers of the fugitive; trace papers, such as credit card receipts; and spend hours in surveillance outside the individual's house, workplace, or another location the fugitive is known to frequent. Bounty hunters can use almost any means possible to catch a fugitive. In most states they can enter a fugitive's home if they believe beyond a reasonable doubt that he or she is inside. Most bounty hunters are licensed to carry weapons. They use them to convince fugitives to return

Bounty Hunters on TV

○ *The Lone Ranger* began airing in 1949 and portrayed a ranger and his sidekick Tonto cleaning up the Old West.

○ *Bounty Hunter* aired in the late 1950s and showed bounty hunting as a respectable career. Steve McQueen starred in the show.

○ *Gunsmoke* depicted the bounty hunter as lawless. The main character, Matt Dillon, often was up against the ruthless bounty hunter.

○ *Walker, Texas Ranger* showed a modern-day ranger (played by Chuck Norris), an updated version of the original Texas Rangers who tracked down lawbreakers in the Texas territory.

EXPLORING

○ Since bounty hunting can be dangerous, it will be difficult to explore this career until you are older and have some experience in law enforcement.

○ You can start learning about bounty hunting by reading books like *Private Investigators and Bounty Hunters* by Ann Gaines (New York: Chelsea House Publishers, 1999) and *Bounty Hunters, Marshals, and Sheriffs: Forward to the Past* by Jacqueline Pope (Westport, Conn.: Praeger Publishers, 1998).

○ Contact your local and state authorities and ask for information about current laws and how they affect bounty hunters.

○ Contact a bail bondsman (you'll find many listed in the phone book) and find out if they are also bounty hunters. Ask any questions you may have. Try to interview several bondsmen to get a more balanced view of what it's like to work in the bail bonding and fugitive recovery business.

peacefully and to protect themselves in case the fugitive becomes violent. Once they find the fugitive, the bounty hunter arrests the individual and takes him or her back to jail to await trial. Some bounty hunters locate the fugitive and then alert the local law officials to make the actual arrest.

Bounty hunters spend much of their time traveling in search of a fugitive or waiting for hours for a fugitive to appear. Because catching a fugitive is easiest in the middle of the night or early morning, the bounty hunter keeps odd hours and may work especially long hours when close to capturing a fugitive.

Education and Training

High school classes in business, communications, government, and political science will help you prepare for the legal and business side of bounty hunting. Taking self-defense or martial arts courses will provide you with the physical skills you might need when capturing a fugitive. Studying a foreign language, such as Spanish, will help you deal with fugitives who do not speak English.

Bounty hunters do not need a college education, but they should have training in law enforcement and criminal justice. Some bounty hunters have a degree in criminal justice or past experience as police officers.

It's a Fact

The history of the bail process dates back to English common law beginning around 1066. People who were charged with crimes against the king were allowed to go free if someone else guaranteed that the individual would return. If that didn't happen, the person who guaranteed the return of the individual often had to pay the price instead.

In America, this process continued and those who offered guarantees for the accused people became known as bail bondsmen and bounty hunters. They worked together to ensure that accused people appeared for hearings, trials, and sentences.

Bounty hunting grew as a profession during the westward expansion of the United States. Fugitives would often run as far west as possible to get away from local law enforcement, so bounty hunters were often found tracking lawbreakers in the Old West.

Groups of men, called Rangers, gathered to clean up areas of the West, such as Arizona and Texas, as they became part of the Union. These men would "range" over large territories, tracking down and apprehending lawbreakers. Later, most bounty-hunting activities were performed by marshals, sheriffs, and detectives.

Earnings

Beginning bounty hunters earn $20,000 or more per year, according to the National Center for Policy Analysis. Experienced bounty hunters who own their own businesses can

Famous Bounty Hunters

○ Pat Garrett tracked down Billy the Kid.
○ Bat Masterson assisted Federal Marshal Wyatt Earp in bringing law and order to Tombstone, Arizona, in the 1880s.
○ The Texas Rangers "thinned out" more than 3,000 Texas desperados in the 1870s.
○ The Arizona Rangers cleaned up the lawlessness of Arizona so that it could become the forty-eighth state of the United States.

FOR MORE INFO

For industry information, contact the following organizations:

American Bail Enforcement Association
PO Box 33244
Austin, TX 78764-0244
Tel: 512-719-3595
http://www.pimall.com/nais/n.dm.html

National Association of Bail Enforcement Agents
PO Box 129
Falls Church, VA 22040-0129
Tel: 703-534-4211
http://www.nabea.org

National Enforcement Agency
PO Box 3540
Gaithersburg, MD 20885-3540
Tel: 866-384-4848
http://nationalbailenforcement.com

National Institute of Bail Enforcement
PO Box 667
Spring Grove, IL 60081-0667
Tel: 815-675-0260
http://www.bounty-hunter.net

make more than $30,000 per year. Bounty hunters generally earn between $40,000 and $60,000 per year, according to CNNMoney. It's important to note, however, that in this business earnings can vary greatly from month to month, depending on how many fugitives the bounty hunter is able to capture, the bail bond for these fugitives, and expenses incurred in the process. Established bounty hunters with excellent reputations often get the highest-paying cases, such as for a fugitive who has run on a $100,000 bail. Their yearly earnings may approach $100,000.

Outlook

Employment for bounty hunters will increase about as fast as the average. Many people want to become bounty hunters, which has created strong competition in the field. Bounty hunters are a small but important part of our legal system and will continue to be needed in the future.

Corrections Officers

What Corrections Officers Do

Corrections officers guard people who have been arrested and are awaiting trial. They also guard those who have been tried, found guilty, and sentenced to prison time. They search prisoners and their cells for weapons and drugs. They check locks, bars on windows and doors, and gates for signs of tampering.

Prisoners must be under guard at all times. Corrections officers count prisoners from time to time to make sure they are all present. Some officers are stationed at gates and on towers to prevent escapes. Corrections officers carefully observe inmates and watch for potential conflicts. The officers try to settle disputes before they erupt into violence. When a disturbance or crime occurs at the prison, officers are responsible for stopping it.

Corrections officers give work assignments to prisoners and supervise them as they work. Sometimes they may check prisoners' mail for forbidden items. If a prisoner is injured, corrections officers give first aid. When visitors come to the prison, officers check their identification before taking them to the visiting area.

Education and Training

Corrections officers generally must be at least 18 to 21 years old and have a high school diploma. Many positions require some postsecondary education or related

Federal Prison Facts, October 2007

- number of institutions: 114
- total inmate population: 200,127
- inmates in minimum security: 17.9 percent
- inmates in low security: 38.5 percent
- inmates in medium security: 28.1 percent
- inmates in high security: 10.9 percent
- number of male inmates: 186,560 (93.2 percent)
- number of female inmates: 13,567 (6.8 percent)
- average inmate age: 38

Source: Federal Bureau of Prisons

EXPLORING

○ Read books about crime, prisons, and law enforcement.

○ Many corrections Web sites have forums for corrections officers and other public safety employees. Visit these Web sites to read about and communicate with people active in this career.

○ Because of age requirements and the nature of the work, there are no opportunities for students to gain actual experience while still in school. Once you turn 18, you can prepare for employment by taking college courses in criminal justice or police science.

work experience. Most states and some local governments train corrections officers on the job. Trainees spend two to six months under the supervision of experienced officers. The federal government and some states have special schools for training corrections officers in programs that last from four to eight weeks.

In many states, you must pass physical fitness, vision, and hearing tests. Some states require one or two years of experience in corrections or related police work.

Earnings

Wages for corrections officers vary considerably depending on their employers and their level of experience. According to the U.S. Department of Labor,

We've Come a Long Way

For centuries, punishment for criminal behavior was generally left in the hands of the injured individual or his or her relatives. This resulted in blood feuds, which could carry on for years. When kingdoms emerged as the standard form of government, the king assumed the responsibility for punishing the wrongs committed by a subject or a clan. In this way, crime became a public offense. The earliest corrections officers were more likely to be executioners and torturers than guards or jailers because jailing criminals was considered a temporary measure until punishment could be carried out.

Early criminals were treated inhumanely. They were often put to death for minor offenses, exiled, forced into hard labor, given corporal punishment, tortured, mutilated, enslaved, or left to rot in dungeons.

mean annual earnings for corrections officers employed by the federal government were $48,000 in 2006; state governments, $38,960; and local governments, $37,330. Salaries for all corrections officers ranged from less than $23,600 to more than $58,580.

Outlook

Employment in this field is expected to increase more slowly than the average, according to the U.S. Department of Labor. Despite this prediction, there should be good opportunities. The war on illegal drugs, new tough-on-crime laws, and increasing mandatory sentencing policies will create a need for more prisons and more corrections officers.

The increasing use of private companies and privately run prisons may somewhat limit the growth of jobs in this field; these companies are more likely to have limited operating budgets, so they typically hire fewer corrections officers. Use of new technologies, such as surveillance equipment, automatic gates, and other devices, may also allow institutions to employ fewer officers.

FOR MORE INFO

For information on careers, contact the following organizations:
American Correctional Association
206 North Washington Street, Suite 200
Alexandria, VA 22314-2528
Tel: 703-224-0000
http://www.aca.org

For information on entrance requirements, training, and career opportunities for corrections officers at the federal level, contact
Federal Bureau of Prisons
320 First Street NW
Washington, DC 20534
Tel: 202-307-3198
E-mail: info@bop.gov
http://www.bop.gov

For information about the corrections industry, visit
Corrections Connection Network News
http://www.corrections.com

Crime Analysts

What Crime Analysts Do

Crime analysts try to find and piece together information about crime patterns, crime trends, and criminal suspects. A crime analyst collects crime data from many sources. Sources include police reports, statewide computer databases, and interviews with suspects. Crime analysts also study general factors such as population density (the number of people in a given area), economic conditions (average income and job availability), and crime-reporting practices. They then analyze this information. Crime analysts are constantly on the lookout for details that may create patterns. These patterns can help them track and predict criminal activity.

This work changes daily. One day, for example, an analyst may meet with the police chief to discuss a string of local car thefts. Another day the analyst may work at the computer, gathering statistics. Sometimes the work includes going on "ride-alongs" with street cops or visiting a crime scene. Crime analysts also sometimes meet with analysts from surrounding areas to exchange information. Occasionally, a crime analyst may be pulled off everyday duties to work exclusively on a task force, usually focusing on a cluster of violent crimes. Crime analysts also monitor the activities of people with criminal reputations, or known offenders. An example of a known offender is a criminal on parole.

Where Do They Work?

- ○ local and state law enforcement agencies
- ○ federal agencies (such as the Federal Bureau of Investigation; U.S. Secret Service; Bureau of Alcohol, Tobacco, and Firearms; U.S. Customs and Border Protection; and U.S. Department of Justice)
- ○ private security firms
- ○ insurance companies
- ○ major retailers

There are three types of analysis: *tactical, strategic,* and *administrative.* Tactical crime analysis provides police officers and detectives with fast, relevant information. This is the type of "hot" information that allows police to set up stakeouts and may lead to the arrest of a criminal. Tactical analysis is also used to identify suspects for certain crimes based on their criminal records.

Strategic analysis deals with finding solutions to long-range problems. For example, an analyst might perform a study to see if the police department is making the best use of its staff. The analyst would then offer suggestions for improvement.

Administrative analysis provides policy-making information to those in charge of a police department. This analysis may include a study on the activity levels of police officers. The results of the study may cause the police department to hire more officers. Administrative work could also include creating graphs and charts that are used in management presentations.

EXPLORING

○ Visit the National Institute of Justice Web site (http://nij.ncjrs.org/publications/pubs_db.asp) to read articles about crime analysis.

○ Although you cannot work as a crime analyst until you are an adult, there are many ways to begin your own training and education now. First, get some exposure to the law enforcement community by volunteering at the local police department. You can also join a program that offers a minicourse on law enforcement.

○ Ask a teacher or guidance counselor to help arrange an information interview with a crime analyst. Ask the following questions: What are your main and secondary job duties? What do you like least and most about your job? How did you train for this field? What advice would you give a young person who is interested in the field?

Education and Training

While you are in high school, you can prepare for a career as a crime analyst by taking English and speech classes that will develop your communication and research skills. Both skills are necessary for this career, since you'll be gathering information and communicating with many different people. Math classes, such as algebra, will help you to understand statistics.

To Be a Successful Crime Analyst, You Should . . .

○ be good with computers
○ be organized
○ be inquisitive, logical, and have an excellent memory for details
○ have solid research skills
○ have a strong stomach for graphic or disturbing crime information
○ be able to work as a member of a law enforcement team

Basic knowledge of computers, word processors, spreadsheets, and databases is also important.

Most agencies that hire crime analysts require that applicants have a bachelor's degree. Many crime analysts have degrees in criminal justice, statistics, computer science, and sociology. A few colleges offer master's degrees or graduate concentrations in crime analysis.

Earnings

Earnings for crime analysts vary considerably, based on factors such as the location, the size of the employing agency and its financial status, and the analyst's experience. The International Association of Crime Analysts reports that salaries range from $25,000 to $60,000 per year.

Outlook

As the job of crime analyst becomes increasingly well known and as analysts' work continues to help the police prevent or solve crimes, the need for these professionals should grow.

The emergence of community-oriented policing is one factor that has increased the need for crime analysts. This type of policing is intended to get police officers to work on the streets of their communities rather than at a desk. To do this, many agencies are hiring civilians for desk jobs, which allows more police officers to have a presence in their community.

The field is also growing because better software is becoming available. While this growth trend is expected to continue, it's important to recognize that it is still a competitive job market. Those who want to become crime analysts should be willing to move to find an agency with a job opening. They should also bear in mind that police departments are historically more likely to lay off a civilian than a street officer.

FOR MORE INFO

For information on careers in criminology, contact
American Society of Criminology
1314 Kinnear Road, Suite 212
Columbus, OH 43212-1156
Tel: 614-292-9207
http://www.asc41.com

For information on careers and useful articles and publications, contact
International Association of Crime Analysts
9218 Metcalf Avenue, #364
Overland Park, KS 66212-1476
Tel: 800-609-3419
http://www.iaca.net

Customs Officials

What Customs Officials Do

Customs officials perform a wide variety of duties including preventing terrorists and terrorist weapons from entering the United States, controlling imports and exports, and combating smuggling and revenue fraud.

As a result of its merger in 2003 with several other protective and monitoring agencies of the U.S. government, U.S. Customs and Border Protection has created a new position, the *Customs and Border Protection (CBP) officer*. These workers are uniformed and armed. A second new position, the *CBP agriculture specialist*, has been created to complement the work of the CBP officer. CBP agriculture specialists are uniformed, but not armed.

CBP officers conduct surveillance at points of entry into the United States to prohibit smuggling, detect customs violations, and deter acts of terrorism. They try to catch people illegally transporting smuggled merchandise and contraband.

CBP officers also are responsible for carefully and thoroughly examining cargo to make sure that it matches the description on a ship's or aircraft's manifest. They inspect baggage and personal items worn or carried by travelers entering or leaving the United States by ship, plane, or automobile.

Facts About CBP Professionals

On an average day in 2006, CBP officials

- processed 1.1 million passengers and pedestrians
- processed 70,900 truck, rail, and sea containers
- executed 63 arrests at ports of entry
- seized 1,769 pounds of illegal narcotics
- seized 4,462 prohibited meat, plant materials, or animal products
- managed 326 ports of entry
- protected more than 6,900 miles of border with Mexico and Canada
- protected 95,000 miles of shoreline

CBP officers examine crew and passenger lists. They sometimes do this in cooperation with police or federal government agencies, who may be searching for criminals or terrorists. They are authorized to search suspicious individuals and to arrest these offenders if necessary.

CBP agriculture specialists inspect agricultural and related goods that are imported into the United States. They help protect people from agroterrorism and bioterrorism, as well as monitor agricultural imports for diseases and harmful pests.

Education and Training

High school courses in government, geography, social studies, English, and history will contribute to your understanding of international and domestic legal issues as well as give you a good general background. If you wish to become a specialist in scientific or investigative aspects of the CBP, courses in the sciences, particularly chemistry, will be necessary and courses in computer science will be helpful. Taking a foreign language, especially Spanish, will also help prepare you for this career.

Applicants to CBP must be U.S. citizens and at least 21 years of age. They must have earned at least a high school diploma, but applicants with college degrees are preferred. Applicants are required to have three years of general work experience involving contact with the public or four years of college. New CBP officers receive 15 weeks of training at

EXPLORING

○ You can learn about the various positions available at CBP by visiting its Web site (http://www.cbp.gov). Additionally, you can read *CBP Today*, the official employee newsletter of U.S. Customs and Border Protection, to learn more about customs work.

○ Another great way to learn more about this career is to participate in the CBP Explorer Program. Applicants must be between the ages of 14 and 21 and have at least a C grade point average in high school or college. Participation in this program is also an excellent starting point for entry into the field. For more information, visit the CBP Web site.

A Customs and Border Protection officer checks a passenger's documents.
(Gerald Nino, U.S. Customs and Border Protection)

the U.S. Customs and Border Protection Academy, which is located at the Federal Law Enforcement Training Center in Glynco, Georgia.

Earnings

Entry-level positions at GS-5 began at a base annual pay of $25,623 in 2007, and entry at GS-7 started at $31,740 per year. Most CBP officers are at the GS-11 position, which had a base annual salary of $46,974 in 2007. Supervisory positions beginning at GS-12 started at $56,301 in 2007. Federal employees in certain cities receive extra locality pay in addition to their salaries to allow for the higher cost of living in those areas.

Outlook

Employment for customs officials is steady and not affected by changes in the economy. There is more emphasis today on law enforcement, especially the deterrence of terrorism, but

Other Opportunities with U.S. Customs and Border Protection

Customs pilots conduct air surveillance of illegal traffic crossing U.S. borders by air, land, or sea.

Canine enforcement officers train and use dogs to prevent smuggling of controlled substances including marijuana, narcotics, and dangerous drugs. Canine enforcement officers also use dogs to detect bomb-making materials or other dangerous substances.

Import specialists are technical experts in a particular line of merchandise, such as wine or electronic equipment. Import specialists routinely question importers, check their lists, and make sure the merchandise matches the description and the list.

Customs and Border Protection chemists protect the health and safety of Americans. They analyze imported merchandise for textile fibers, lead content, narcotics, and presence of explosives or other harmful material.

Criminal investigators, or *special agents,* are plainclothes investigators who make sure that the government obtains revenue on imports and that contraband and controlled substances do not enter or leave the country illegally. They investigate smuggling, criminal fraud, and major cargo thefts.

also the detection of illegally imported drugs and pornography and the prevention of exports of certain high-technology items. This means the prospects for steady employment are good.

FOR MORE INFO

For career information, visit CBP's Web site
U.S. Customs and Border Protection (CBP)
U.S. Department of Homeland Security
1300 Pennsylvania Avenue NW
Washington, DC 20229
Tel: 202-354-1000
http://www.cbp.gov

Deputy U.S. Marshals

What Deputy U.S. Marshals Do

Deputy U.S. marshals are law enforcement officers who protect and enforce the decisions of the U.S. judiciary system. The judiciary system includes judges, the Supreme Court, and the Department of Justice.

Deputy U.S. marshals take federal criminals to prison, sometimes in government-owned aircraft. They are on guard in federal courtrooms and protect judges and jury members who are involved in important legal cases that put their lives in possible danger. They serve subpoenas (a formal request that asks a person to come to court to testify), summonses (a request by a court or other legal authority to appear before the entity), and other legal documents.

Marshals investigate and track down fugitives (criminals who are running from the law), even those who have escaped to another country. They also try to find fugitives in the United States who are wanted by foreign nations. In hunting down fugitives, marshals often work with state and local police departments and with other law enforcement agencies.

The Marshals Service operates the nation's witness relocation program. This program encourages witnesses to testify in federal trials even if they feel that their testimony would put them in

Facts About the U.S. Marshal Service

In 2006, the U.S. Marshal Service:

- ○ arrested more than 38,000 federal fugitives
- ○ conducted more than 349,000 prisoner movements
- ○ protected more than 2,000 federal judges
- ○ provided security for 146 high threat trials
- ○ managed a total of 17,657 people in its Witness Security Program
- ○ received 195,636 prisoners

Inside the U.S. Marshals Service

There are 94 districts across the United States and Puerto Rico, Guam, the Virgin Islands, and the Northern Marianas to which marshals are assigned. Each district is managed by a U.S. marshal, who is appointed by the president. Beneath the marshal is the *chief deputy U.S. marshal,* who directs a staff of supervisors, deputy U.S. marshals, and other support staff. In addition, specialists in witness security, court security, seized property, and enforcement provide professional expertise for each district field office. A total of 3,067 deputy marshals are employed by the U.S. Marshals Service.

danger, such as in organized crime cases. The Marshals Service provides personal protection for the witness until he or she testifies in court. After the trial is over, the Marshals Service helps the witness move to a new city and take on a new name and identity. This keeps him or her anonymous and safe from reprisals.

U.S. marshals also operate the program for confiscating property that has been purchased from the profits of certain illegal activities such as drug dealing. The marshals seize the houses, boats, and other property that criminals have purchased. They hold it and maintain it until the property is sold or put up for auction. Hundreds of millions of dollars in seized assets are in the custody of the Marshals Service.

Marshals are trained to respond to emergency situations such as riots, terrorist attacks, or hostage situations when federal law is violated or federal property is endangered. A highly trained force of deputy U.S. marshals called the Special Operations Group is deployed in these situations.

Education and Training

If you are interested in becoming a deputy U.S. marshal, you must complete high school and earn an undergraduate degree or have at least three years' experience in law enforcement,

EXPLORING

○ For any law enforcement job, it is difficult to obtain practical experience prior to entering the field. If you are interested in more information about working as a deputy U.S. marshal, you should contact the U.S. Marshals Service (http://www.usdoj.gov/marshals).

○ The U.S. Marshals Service has an excellent Web site for kids (http://www.usmarshals.gov/usmsforkids). Visit it to read about a week in the life of a marshal, take quizzes and play word games, become a junior deputy marshal, and much more.

○ Visit http://www.usmarshals.gov/history to read a detailed history of the U.S. Marshals Service.

○ Ask your guidance counselor to help arrange an information interview with a U.S. deputy marshal.

corrections, or other fields. In high school, you should take courses in government, one or more foreign languages, English, history, and computer science.

Like other federal officers, deputy U.S. marshals are trained at the U.S. Marshals Service Training Academy in Glynco, Georgia. They complete a program that teaches them about laws, proper procedures, firearm use, and physical training.

Earnings

As with other federal positions, salaries for deputy U.S. marshals are fixed at government service rating levels. Beginning deputy U.S. marshals are generally hired at the GS-5 level, at which an annual salary was between $25,623 to $33,309 in 2007. Deputy U.S. marshals with bachelor's degrees, and especially those with advanced degrees in law enforcement, criminology, law, and other related disciplines, may be hired at the GS-7 level, which draws a salary between $31,740 and $41,262.

Top salaries for deputy U.S. marshals are at the GS-11 level, which paid a base rate of $46,974 per year in 2007, but deputy U.S. marshals certified in a specialty area may earn the GS-12 level, which was $56,301 in 2007. The top rating, GS-15, paid $93,063 to $120,981 per year in 2007.

To Be a Successful Deputy U.S. Marshal, You Should . . .

○ be in excellent physical condition

○ have good hearing

○ be decisive and calm under pressure

○ have strong organizational skills

○ be willing to work in dangerous situations

Outlook

Careers in law enforcement and security-related fields in general are expected to grow rapidly in many cases. This is because federal and state governments are passing new tough-on-crime legislation and the number of criminals continues to grow. The threat of terrorism has also created an improved job outlook for U.S. marshals. There is now increased security particularly in and around government offices, public buildings, airports, post offices, and media headquarters.

In spite of the continuing need for deputy U.S. marshals, competition for available positions will remain high. Many people want to work in this career and also receive the generous fringe benefits available for many careers in federal service.

FOR MORE INFO

For information on career opportunities, contact

U.S. Marshals Service
Human Resources Division–Law Enforcement Recruiting
Washington, DC 20530-1000
Tel: 202-307-9600
E-mail: us.marshals@usdoj.gov
http://www.usdoj.gov/marshals

Detectives

What Detectives Do

Detectives investigate crimes, gather information for trials and other legal proceedings, help locate missing persons, and serve as bodyguards to important people. To gather information, they conduct research in libraries and on the Internet and interview people in person, via e-mail, or on the telephone. Detectives are sometimes known as *private investigators.*

Private investigators have many of the same duties as police officers. They gather clues from accidents or crime scenes, conduct surveillance of suspects, and check people's personal histories to learn more about their backgrounds. There are two important differences between investigators and police officers: investigators do not have to follow the same legal procedures when they interview suspects and gather evidence, and investigators cannot make arrests. Private detectives sometimes work with police officers to solve crimes.

Private investigators are usually employed by detective agencies. Clients approach these agencies with specific problems. For example, a company might hire an investigator to prevent shoplifting, vandalism, or another type of business crime. Investigators may be asked to look into insurance claims to make sure that people who are claiming property damage or injury have

Popular Specialties

Here are the some of the most popular private investigation specialties:

- insurance claims investigation
- background checks
- locating missing persons
- surveillance
- executive protection
- countermeasures
- fraud investigation
- criminal investigations
- accident investigations

actually had property destroyed or stolen, or have been injured. The detectives conduct an investigation and provide a written or oral account to report findings to their client.

A private investigator's work can lead to the recovery of stolen artwork or a missing child, the arrest of a shoplifter, or the uncovering of a spy operation. But for every success there are many hours of searching for clues. Investigations can be dangerous. Detectives may have to travel to rough neighborhoods late at night to interview witnesses or gather evidence. Suspects may threaten them. Most of the work, however, is safe.

Education and Training

Many people become investigators after working as police officers. There are several detective training programs that prepare you to interview people, research public records, locate missing persons, take fingerprints, pick locks, and operate cameras, hidden microphones, and other surveillance equipment. These programs usually last several months. Students then receive on-the-job training at a detective agency before they become investigators. Most programs only accept high school graduates. Many community colleges and universities offer degree programs in criminal justice or a related field.

Most states require private investigators to take a licensing test. Those who carry a gun usually have to pass an examination to show they know how to use a firearm. Some states

EXPLORING

○ Ask your librarian to help you find books and magazines on detectives.

○ There are few means of exploring the field of detective work, and actual experience in the field prior to employment is unlikely. If you are interested in becoming a private investigator, you should talk with your school guidance counselor, your local police department, local private detective agencies, a private investigation school, or a college or university offering police science, criminal justice, or law enforcement courses.

○ Practice your detective skills by playing board games, such as 221b Baker Street, Clue, 13 Dead End Drive, Murder She Wrote, and Scotland Yard. Additionally, there are many computer games that test your mystery- and puzzle-solving skills.

require an applicant to have law enforcement experience, or to have completed an apprenticeship period with an experienced investigator, in order to obtain a license.

Earnings

Private detectives and investigators had median annual earnings of $33,750 in 2006, according to the U.S. Department of

Trends in Private Investigation

Digital Data Recovery and Computer Crime

More and more data is being stored on computers instead of on paper. As a result, more private investigators are specializing in investigating computer crime and recovering electronic data.

Nursing Homes

More private investigators are working with attorneys to uncover abuse in nursing homes.

Countermeasures

U.S. businesses are losing billions of dollars a year through theft of trade secrets and illegal eavesdropping. Business and industry are hiring private investigators to take countermeasures against these crimes. (For example, they try to locate and confiscate hidden surveillance equipment.)

Premises Liability

Attorneys and private investigators are working together to investigate premises liability, specifically in the area of inadequate security (landlords and businesses failing to provide adequate security).

Domestic Investigations

Divorce investigation has been the primary work for many private investigation agencies since the 1950s. It is still a major trend today. Divorce investigations can involve surveillance and activities checks, child custody and child abuse issues, and the discovery of hidden assets.

Detectives Focus on Kids

A number of private detectives firms now specialize in children's cases. The prevalence of divorce, the increasing use of daily child care, and the awareness of child abuse have led to this specialization, which focuses on these areas:

○ background checks for child care workers
○ background checks on nannies
○ rental of temporary video camera equipment
○ child abuse investigation

Labor. Salaries ranged from less than $19,720 to more than $64,380. Self-employed investigators can earn from $50 to $150 or more an hour.

Outlook

Job opportunities for private detectives are expected to grow faster than the average. Many people leave this profession due to the long hours and possible danger. This will create many openings for detectives. Hotels, insurance firms, restaurants, and other businesses are hiring more private investigators. Private investigators who specialize in computer fraud should have very strong employment opportunities.

FOR MORE INFO

For industry information, contact
National Association of Investigative Specialists
PO Box 82148
Austin, TX 78708-2148
Tel: 512-719-3595
http://www.pimall.com/nais/nais.j.html

For information on certification, contact
National Association of Legal Investigators
235 North Pine Street
Lansing, MI 48933-1021
Tel: 866-520-6254
http://www.nalionline.org

FBI Agents

What FBI Agents Do

The Federal Bureau of Investigation (FBI) is a government agency that trains special agents or investigators to investigate people who are suspected of crimes against the United States. *FBI agents* also track down criminals who have broken federal laws. These crimes include terrorism, computer crime, bank robbery, kidnapping, theft, spying against the United States (espionage), and destroying U.S. property (sabotage). The FBI is responsible for investigating more than 200 violations of federal law.

Agents send their reports and the evidence from their investigations to the criminal laboratory at the FBI head-quarters in Washington, D.C. There they are filed in various

Words to Learn

The Bureau the Federal Bureau of Investigation

method of operation (M.O.) the standard pattern someone uses to commit a crime

profile a general description of a type of person who might commit a certain kind of crime; for example, the FBI creates profiles of serial killers, financial criminals, and terrorists

special agent a government title for federal employees who investigate criminal violations

street agent an FBI agent who conducts investigations

surveillance to gather information by following, observing, or listening to people

wiretap electronic surveillance over the telephone

departments such as fingerprinting, firearms, documents, or photography. This information is available to any law enforcement agency in the United States.

The work of FBI agents is top secret and often dangerous. Agents cannot talk about their assignments with family or friends. They often work alone, but they keep in touch with law enforcement agencies all over the world. Their travels take them to a variety of cities where they may investigate people and take part in arrests and raids.

Unlike police officers, agents wear ordinary clothes so they will not draw attention to themselves. They usually carry some form of identification so others will know they are acting on behalf of the U.S. government. Those who do dangerous work carry guns for protection.

Education and Training

The FBI does not recommend specific courses for high school students. Rather, the bureau encourages students to do the best work they can. Since FBI agents perform a variety of work, numerous academic disciplines are needed.

To become an FBI agent, you must be a citizen of the United States and be at least 23 years old. You need at least one of the following: a degree from a

New agents at the FBI Training Academy in Quantico, Virginia, learn defensive techniques. (Rob Crandall, The Image Works)

EXPLORING

○ One great way to learn more about a career as an FBI agent is to visit the FBI's Kids' Page (http://www.fbi.gov/fbikids.htm).

○ Ask your librarian to help you find books and other resources on the FBI and crime fighting. Here are some suggestions: *The FBI*, by Sarah De Capua (New York: Children's Press, 2007); *Crime Scene: How Investigators Use Science to Track Down the Bad Guys,* 2d ed., by Vivien Bowers (Toronto: Maple Tree Press, 2006); and *Forensic Science*, by Ron Fridell (Minneapolis, Minn.: Lerner Publications, 2006).

○ Ask your teacher to arrange an information interview with an FBI agent.

Fingerprint Facts

The fingerprint section of the FBI Laboratory is the largest in the world. It has developed computer technology called the Integrated Automated Fingerprint Identification System that houses more than 46 million digital sets of fingerprints. The lab

○ identifies and maintains fingerprint records for arrested criminal suspects, government employees, and applicants for federal jobs
○ posts notices about people wanted for crimes and for parole or probation violations
○ examines physical evidence for fingerprints and provides court testimony on examination results
○ trains agents in fingerprint science
○ keeps fingerprint records of missing persons
○ identifies amnesia victims and unknown deceased people

law school; fluency in a foreign language; or a bachelor's degree in accounting, economics, business, finance, engineering, or computer science. If your degree is in another subject, you need three years of full-time work experience after college or a graduate degree and two to three years of work experience.

New agents complete an extensive 18-week training program at the FBI Academy at Quantico, Virginia. There they learn FBI rules and regulations, fingerprinting, firearm techniques, defensive tactics, and federal criminal law. After training, new agents are put on probation for a year. During this time a senior agent supervises them. If they are found to be fit after a year, the new agents are hired permanently.

Earnings

New FBI agents start out at the federal government's GS-10 level—approximately $42,755 in 2007, depending on where the agent lives. FBI agents who do not manage other agents can reach the GS-13 grade—about $66,951 in 2007. Agents who move into management positions can earn a GS-15 salary—about $93,063. Some agents then move into a different employment category called the Senior Executive Service, where they make more than $100,000 annually working for the FBI.

Outlook

Increases in organized crime, white-collar crime, and terrorist threats on American soil have led the FBI to increase the number of agents in recent years. Job vacancies also open up as agents retire, advance, or resign, but turnover is low because most agents stay with the FBI throughout their working lives. Competition for openings is extremely strong.

FOR MORE INFO

For information about a career as an FBI agent, contact a local field office or visit the FBI's Web site

Federal Bureau of Investigation (FBI)
J. Edgar Hoover Building
935 Pennsylvania Avenue NW
Washington, DC 20535-0001
Tel: 202-324-3000
http://www.fbi.gov

Fire Inspectors and Investigators

What Fire Inspectors and Investigators Do

Most fire departments are responsible for fire prevention activities. *Fire inspectors* inspect buildings and their storage contents for rubbish, chemicals, and other materials that can ignite, or start on fire, easily. They look for worn-out or exposed wiring and electrical code violations. Fire inspectors also examine a facility's fire protection equipment, such as sprinkler systems, alarms, and fire extinguishers, to make sure that they are functioning properly. While inspecting buildings, they might make recommendations on how fire safety equipment could be placed or used better. They provide information regarding the storage of flammable materials, electrical hazards, and other common causes of fires.

Fire inspectors pay close attention to public buildings, such as hospitals, schools, nursing homes, theaters, restaurants, and hotels, which they inspect regularly. They also review evacuation plans and monitor fire drills to make sure the plans are effective.

Inspectors review plans for new buildings to make sure they incorporate fire suppression and alarm systems that are adequate and conform to government safety codes.

Fire Facts, 2006

- 3,245 civilians died and 16,400 civilians were injured as a result of fire.
- 89 firefighters were killed in the line of duty.
- More than 1.6 million fires were reported.
- 31,000 fires were intentionally set, causing 305 civilian deaths and an estimated $755 million in property damage.

Source: National Fire Protection Association

Inspectors maintain reports and records related to fire inspections, code requirements, permits, and training. They also instruct employers, civic groups, schoolchildren, and others on how to extinguish small fires, escape burning buildings, operate fire extinguishers, and establish evacuation plans.

Fire investigators, or *fire marshals,* try to find the causes of fires. Once fires are out, or extinguished, investigators determine the fuel and heat sources that caused the fires. They determine whether the fire was incendiary (deliberately set, or arson) or accidental. If the fires are of suspicious origin or caused death or injury, investigators look for more evidence of arson. Fire investigators interrogate witnesses, obtain statements and other necessary documentation, and preserve and examine evidence. They tour fire scenes and prepare comprehensive reports of investigative procedures.

Fire investigators submit reports to a district attorney (a special type of lawyer who works for the government), testify in court, or, if they have police authority, arrest suspected arsonists. Investigators also gather information from accidental fires to determine where and how the fire started and how it spread.

> ## Types of Fires
>
> Approximately 1,642,500 fires occurred in the United States in 2006. Of these:
>
> ○ 51.2 percent were outside and other fires
> ○ 31.9 percent were structure fires
> ○ 16.9 percent were vehicle fires
>
> Source: National Fire Protection Association

Education and Training

Earning a high school diploma is the first step to becoming a fire inspector or investigator. Take classes in physics, biology, and mathematics. Speech and English courses will help you polish your communication skills.

There are two ways to become a fire inspector. Some fire departments have policies that only those who have served as firefighters can work in the fire prevention bureau. Other

EXPLORING

○ Become familiar with fire safety and science by visiting the fire safety and education section of the U.S. Fire Administration's Web site (http://www.usfa.dhs.gov/citizens). Also visit the U.S. Fire Administration's Web page at http://www.usfa.dhs.gov.

○ Your school guidance counselor or a teacher can help arrange for a visit to a local fire department for a tour of the facilities, where you may also have the opportunity to talk with firefighters about their work. An information interview with a fire inspector or investigator can also provide you with insights.

○ Many fire departments have volunteer programs. Find out if there are any in your area and sign up to volunteer if you meet their requirements.

○ You can also add to your skills by taking CPR and first-aid classes.

departments want people who are trained primarily for fire prevention. Either way, if you want to join the fire department, you should take a two- or four-year college program in fire service, fire protection, and fire-protection systems and equipment. Specialized fire prevention classes required for inspectors, such as hazardous materials and processes, flammable liquids, and high-piled stock, are offered by colleges or the state fire marshal's office.

Fire investigators must have knowledge of fire science, chemistry, engineering, and investigative techniques. A background in law enforcement is helpful.

Earnings

Inspector salaries depend on two things: if they work in the public or private sector and how large those departments or companies are. Typical starting salaries range from $30,000 to $45,000 to $75,000 and can increase with experience and years with the organization.

Fire inspectors and investigators earned a median annual salary of $48,050 in 2006, according to the U.S. Department of Labor. Those just starting out earned less than $29,840, while those with considerable experience earned $74,930 or more. Fire inspectors and investigators in local government jobs earned approximately $51,320 a year.

To Be a Successful Fire Investigator, You Should . . .

- ○ be organized
- ○ be attentive to detail
- ○ be in good physical condition to adapt to extreme weather or fire scene conditions
- ○ have good vision
- ○ have integrity
- ○ have strong communication skills in order to convey your findings in court and in writing

Outlook

The outlook for fire inspectors is about the same as it is for firefighters. Employment should grow faster than the average. Fire investigators have an even better employment outlook than fire inspectors, since there will always be fires to investigate. This field is constantly being advanced by new technology and is one of the most interesting aspects of the fire service.

FOR MORE INFO

For information on the investigation of arson, contact
International Association of Arson Investigators
2151 Priest Bridge Drive, Suite 25
Crofton, MD 21114-2466
Tel: 410-451-3473
http://www.firearson.com/insideiaai/
featuredtopics/index.asp

For information on fire safety issues, careers in fire protection, and public education, contact

National Fire Protection Association
One Batterymarch Park
Quincy, MA 02169-7471
Tel: 617-770-3000
http://www.nfpa.org

For statistics on firefighting, contact
U.S. Fire Administration
16825 South Seton Avenue
Emmitsburg, MD 21727-8920
Tel: 301-447-1000
http://www.usfa.dhs.gov/nfa

Firefighters

What Firefighters Do

Firefighters protect people and their property from fire and other emergencies. They put out fires in many types of locations, including homes, schools, and office buildings. When a fire department receives an emergency call, firefighters are ready to perform their assigned duties. One group of firefighters may be assigned to raise ladders and connect hoses to water hydrants. Others may be asked to break down doors or windows so that others can enter the area with water hoses. Some firefighters are tasked with finding and rescuing people who are trapped in a fire. Most firefighters are also trained to provide emergency medical assistance, such as CPR. Commanding officers such as fire captains, battalion chiefs, or the fire chief coordinate and supervise these activities.

Some firefighters, called *fire inspectors,* conduct safety inspections to look for fire dangers and unsafe conditions. They visit public buildings, such as hospitals, theaters, schools, nursing homes, and hotels, to check for faulty wiring and other fire hazards. Inspectors also make sure that sprinkler systems and other fire-prevention equipment are working properly. If they find problems, they instruct the building's owner to fix them.

After a fire has been struck, or put out, specially trained firefighters called *fire investigators* try to find out what

It's a Fact

○ Today, there are more than 30,000 organized fire departments across the United States, with about 282,000 professional, salaried firefighters.

○ Fire departments responded to an estimated 1,642,500 fires in 2006. These fires resulted in 89 firefighter deaths, 3,245 civilian fire fatalities, 16,400 civilian fire injuries, and more than $11.3 billion in property loss.

Source: National Fire Protection Association

Firefighters need to be calm, decisive, and brave during potentially life-threatening situations. (First Light, Corbis)

caused it. If fire investigators find that a fire was set deliberately, they gather the evidence that proves this and provides clues about who set the fire, arrest the suspected arsonist, and testify in court.

Between emergency calls, firefighters keep the firefighting equipment in good working order. They repair their protective gear, test their oxygen tanks to ensure that they are working properly, oil and polish mechanical equipment, and dry and stretch hoses into shape. They participate in practice drills to become better at firefighting procedures. Fire inspectors and investigators take classes and learn about new technologies in order to keep their skills up to date.

Major Causes of Home Fires, 2000–2004

- cooking equipment: 32 percent
- heating equipment: 16 percent
- arson: 5 percent
- candle: 4 percent
- smoking materials: 4 percent
- exposure to other fire: 4 percent
- confined or contained trash or rubbish fire: 4 percent
- electrical distribution or lighting equipment: 3 percent
- clothing dryer or washer: 2 percent
- people playing with heat source: 2 percent

Source: National Fire Protection Association

EXPLORING

○ Take classes in first aid and CPR. Your community may offer these training courses. Also contact the Boy Scouts of America or the American Red Cross chapter in your area for information on classes.

○ Volunteer for any fire prevention activities offered at your school. Many teachers appoint a student "fire marshal" who is in charge of leading classmates to the proper exits during fire drills and real fire emergencies.

○ Does your family have an evacuation plan for fire emergencies? Talk to your parents about what to do if a fire should start in your home. Discuss various exit routes and assign specific tasks for each family member, such as calling 911 or helping a grandparent or toddler get out of the house safely.

Firefighters often work long shifts, spending many hours at a time in the station. They must be prepared to answer an alarm call at any moment. In many smaller towns, they may be employed on a part-time basis or serve as volunteers. This means that they are on alarm call from their homes, and sometimes they have to leave during a family meal or in the middle of the night.

Education and Training

A high school diploma is the minimum educational requirement to enter the field in most towns and cities. Classes in sciences such as anatomy, biology, chemistry, and physics will provide you with a general background for the field.

Firefighters employed by larger cities must have some postsecondary education. Many people who plan to become firefighters attend two-year postsecondary fire-technology programs, which are offered at junior and community colleges. Beginning firefighters receive several weeks of intensive training, either on the job or through formal fire department training schools. This training covers city laws and ordinances, fire prevention, first aid, and the use and care of equipment. Applicants usually must pass written tests and meet certain requirements for height, weight, physical fitness, stamina, and vision. Firefighters must be at least 18 years old.

Earnings

Full-time firefighters who were just starting out in the field averaged about $20,660 a year in 2006, according to the U.S. Department of Labor. Experienced firefighters earned salaries that ranged from $41,190 to $66,140 or more a year. Fire inspectors and investigators earned salaries that ranged from $29,840 to $74,930 or more in 2006. For all positions, earnings vary with the size of the fire department and the location.

Outlook

Employment of firefighters is expected to grow faster than the average, according to the U.S. Department of Labor, as new firefighters are needed to replace those who retire or leave the field for other reasons. Firefighting is forecasted to remain a very competitive field, and the number of people interested in becoming firefighters will be higher than the number of available positions in most areas.

FOR MORE INFO

For information on careers in the fire service, contact
International Association of Fire Fighters
1750 New York Avenue NW, Suite 300
Washington, DC 20006-5395
Tel: 202-737-8484
http://www.iaff.org

For information on fire safety issues, careers in fire protection, and public education, contact
National Fire Protection Association
One Batterymarch Park
Quincy, MA 02169-7471
Tel: 617-770-3000
http://www.nfpa.org

Forensic Experts

What Forensic Experts Do

Forensic experts, also called *criminalists,* examine physical evidence of crimes. They use spectroscopes, microscopes, gas chromatographs, infrared and ultraviolet light, microphotography, and other lab measuring and testing equipment to analyze fibers, fabric, dust, soils, paint chips, glass fragments, fire accelerants, paper and ink, and other substances in order to identify their composition and origin. They analyze poisons, drugs, and other substances found in bodies by examining tissue samples, stomach contents, and blood samples. They analyze and classify blood, blood alcohol, semen, hair, fingernails, teeth, human and animal bones and tissue, and other biological specimens. Using samples of the genetic material DNA, they can match a person with a sample of body tissue. They study documents to determine whether they are forged or genuine. They also examine the physical properties of firearms, bullets, and explosives.

At the scene of a crime, forensic experts collect and label evidence. They search for spent bullets or bits of an exploded bomb and other objects scattered by an explosion. They look for footprints, fingerprints, and tire tracks, which must be recorded or preserved by plaster casting before they are wiped out. Forensic experts take notes and

Forensic Science Specialties

The following forensic science specialties are recognized by the American Academy of Forensic Sciences:

- ○ criminalistics
- ○ engineering sciences
- ○ jurisprudence
- ○ odontology
- ○ pathology and biology
- ○ physical anthropology
- ○ psychiatry and behavioral science
- ○ questioned documents
- ○ toxicology

photographs to preserve the arrangement of objects, bodies, and debris.

Fingerprint classifiers catalog and compare fingerprints of suspected criminals with records to determine if the people who left the fingerprints at the scene of a crime were involved in previous crimes. They often try to match the fingerprints of unknown corpses with fingerprint records to establish their identity. *Identification technicians* handle fingerprint records and also work with police reports and eyewitness information about crimes and accidents. *Forensic pathologists* perform autopsies to determine the cause of death. *Forensic psychiatrists* conduct psychiatric evaluations of accused criminals and are often called to testify on whether the accused is mentally fit to stand trial. *Molecular biologists* and *geneticists* analyze and review forensic and paternity samples. *Forensic toxicologists* detect and identify the presence of poisons or drugs in a victim's body. *Forensic odontologists* use dental records and evidence to identify crime victims and to investigate bite marks. *Forensic anthropologists* examine and identify bones and skeletal remains.

EXPLORING

○ Visit the American Academy of Forensic Sciences Web site, which offers a useful resource called *So You Want to Be a Forensic Scientist!* (http://www.aafs.org).

○ Read both fiction and nonfiction crime mysteries, and note how crime solvers collect and study evidence. Check out: *Crime Scene: How Investigators Use Science to Track Down the Bad Guys* by Vivian Bowers (Toronto: Maple Tree Press, 2006, and *Forensic Science*, by Ron Fridell (Minneapolis, Minn.: Lerner Publications, 2006).

○ Participating in science clubs will help you become familiar with using microscopes and improve your skills of observation.

Education and Training

Courses in computers, mathematics, the physical sciences, photography, and English are good preparation for a career in forensics.

For some experts, such as identification technicians, the minimum requirement is a high school diploma. On-the-job

A forensic expert tests filter paper for bodily fluids. (Jim Craigmyle, Corbis)

training is then provided. If you are interested in one of the more technical fields, you will need a bachelor's, master's, or even a doctoral degree. A number of universities and community colleges in the United States offer programs in forensic science, pathology, and various aspects of crime lab work. Courses in anatomy, physiology, chemistry, and biology are necessary. For medical examiners, a medical degree is required.

Earnings

Earnings for forensic experts vary according to the type of employer, in what area of the United States the individual works, and a person's educational and skill levels. Salaries for entry-level positions as research assistants or technicians working in local and regional labs range from $20,000 to $25,000. Individuals with a bachelor's degree and two to five years of specialized experience earn salaries that range from $30,000 to $40,000. Salaries for those with advanced degrees range from $50,000 to more than $100,000 a year. The U.S. Department of Labor reports that the median salary for forensic science technicians was $45,330 in 2006.

Outlook

Employment for forensic experts is expected to grow much faster than the average, according to the U.S. Department of Labor. Population increases, rising crime rates, and the greater emphasis on scientific methodology in crime investigation will

To Be a Successful Forensic Expert, You Should . . .

○ have good communication skills, including strong writing skills in order to prepare scientific reports

○ be an excellent note-taker

○ be able to make precise measurements and observations

○ have a good memory

○ have a curious nature

○ have integrity

○ be logical

○ be able to work as a member of a team

likely increase the need for trained experts. Forensic experts with a bachelor's degree in forensic science or a related field will enjoy the best employment prospects.

FOR MORE INFO

For information on careers and colleges and universities that offer forensic science programs, contact
American Academy of Forensic Sciences
410 North 21st Street
Colorado Springs, CO 80904-2712
Tel: 719-636-1100
http://www.aafs.org

To learn more about forensic services at the FBI, visit the FBI Laboratory Division's Web site.
Federal Bureau of Investigation (FBI)
J. Edgar Hoover Building
935 Pennsylvania Avenue NW
Washington, DC 20535-0001

Tel: 202-324-3000
http://www.fbi.gov

For additional information on forensics and forensics professionals, contact the following organizations.
American Society of Questioned Document Examiners
http://www.asqde.org

Society of Forensic Toxicologists
One MacDonald Center
One North MacDonald Street, Suite 15
Mesa, AZ 85201-7340
Tel: 888-866-7638
E-mail: office@soft-tox.org
http://www.soft-tox.org

Health and Regulatory Inspectors

What Health and Regulatory Inspectors Do

In the United States, the government passes laws to protect the health and safety of the public. *Health and regulatory inspectors* enforce those laws. Some health and regulatory inspectors work for the federal government. Others work for state and local governments. These inspectors have different

The Agency Maze

Numerous local, state, and federal agencies oversee the many areas of inspection and regulation. One major agency is the U.S. Department of Health and Human Services, which was formed in 1953. One of its main operating components is the Public Health Service, which operates a number of health and regulatory subagencies including the Food and Drug Administration and the National Institutes of Health.

Other agencies involved with health and regulatory inspection include:

Citizenship and Immigration Services

Customs and Border Protection

Department of Agriculture

Department of the Interior

Environmental Protection Agency

Occupational Safety and Health Administration

Postal Service

titles depending on the type of work they do. There are many different types of inspectors.

Agricultural inspectors make sure that we receive reliable and safe fruits, vegetables, grains, and dairy products. They check not only domestic products but also products shipped to the United States from foreign countries. Some of these inspectors check aircraft, ships, and railway cars to make sure that no illegal products enter the United States.

Customs and Border Protection officers prevent terrorists and terrorist weapons from entering the United States, control imports and exports, and combat smuggling and revenue fraud.

EXPLORING

○ If you are interested in work as a health or regulatory inspector, you may learn more by talking with people who are employed as inspectors and with your high school counselor.

○ Employment in a specific field during summer vacations could be valuable preparation and an opportunity to determine if a general field, such as food preparation, is of interest to you.

Environmental health inspectors enforce standards of cleanliness in food processing plants, restaurants, hospitals, and other industries. They make sure that food is safe, garbage is disposed of properly, and water and air quality meet government standards.

Food and drug inspectors check companies that produce, store, handle, and market food, drugs, and cosmetics. They use scales, thermometers, chemical testing kits, ultraviolet lights, and cameras. They look for evidence to determine whether a product is harmful to the public's health or does not meet other standards for safety.

Occupational safety and health inspectors are responsible for the safety and health of employees in the workplace. They inspect machinery, working conditions, and equipment to make sure that proper safety precautions are used. They monitor noise and air pollution, chemical exposure, and hazardous waste.

To Be a Successful Health and Regulatory Inspector, You Should . . .

- ○ be precision minded
- ○ have an eye for detail
- ○ be responsible
- ○ be able to work as a member of a team
- ○ be tenacious and patient in order to follow each case from investigation to its conclusion
- ○ be able to write effective reports that convey vast amounts of information and investigative work

Education and Training

If you want to become a health and regulatory inspector, you must earn a bachelor's degree. High school courses that are good preparation include biology, health, chemistry, agriculture, earth sciences, and shop.

Health and regulatory inspectors are highly trained professionals who must have excellent knowledge of federal, state, and local laws. In addition, some inspectors have to pass written examinations relating to the type of inspections they will perform.

Earnings

Most federally employed health and regulatory inspectors receive starting salaries that range from $25,000 to $32,000. The median annual salary for all inspectors is approximately $40,000. Some earn more than $75,000 a year.

Salaries vary depending on the job title. For example, inspectors for consumer safety earn $40,000, customs officers earn $46,000, quality assurance inspectors earn $52,000, occupational safety and health inspectors earn about $55,000, and environmental health specialists earn $60,000 a year. Health and regulatory inspectors for state and local governments generally earn salaries lower than those paid by the federal government.

Outlook

Employment for health and regulatory inspectors is likely to grow about as fast as the average, according to the U.S. Department of Labor. There is growing public concern for the environment, safety, and the quality of products.

FOR MORE INFO

For additional information, contact:
Environmental Protection Agency
1200 Pennsylvania Avenue NW
Washington, DC 20460
http://www.epa.gov

Occupational Safety and Health Administration
U.S. Department of Labor
200 Constitution Avenue NW
Washington, DC 20210-0002
http://www.osha.gov

U.S. Customs and Border Protection (CBP)
U.S. Department of Homeland Security
1300 Pennsylvania Avenue NW
Washington, DC 20229
Tel: 202-354-1000
http://www.cbp.gov

U.S. Department of Agriculture
1400 Independence Avenue SW
Washington, DC 20250-0003
http://www.usda.gov

U.S. Department of Health and Human Services
200 Independence Avenue SW
Washington, DC 20201-0007
http://phs.os.dhhs.gov/phs

Park Rangers

What Park Rangers Do

Park rangers protect animals and preserve forests, lakes, grasslands, deserts, and other natural resources in national and state parks. They teach visitors about the park by giving lectures and tours. They also make sure that visitors follow rules and regulations. These might include instructions not to drive off park roads, not to collect rocks or plants, and not to walk too close to dangerous wild animals such as buffalo and mountain lions. Following these rules keeps visitors safe, while protecting natural and cultural resources. Park rangers must also deal with more serious offenses such as assault, murder, and drug smuggling. The National Park Service is one of the major employers of park rangers. In addition, park rangers are employed by other federal land and resource management agencies and similar state and local agencies.

The safety of visitors is one of the main concerns of park rangers. Rangers often require visitors to register at park offices so they will know when the visitors are expected to return from a hike or other activity. Rangers are trained in first aid and, if there is an accident, they may need to help visitors who have been injured. Rangers carefully mark hiking trails and other areas to reduce the risk of injuries for visitors and to protect plants and animals.

Rangers help visitors enjoy and learn about parks. They give lectures and provide guided tours of the park, explaining why certain plants and animals live there. They discuss the rocks and soil in the area and point out important historical sites.

Park rangers also conduct research. They might study wildlife behavior by tagging, or marking, and following certain animals. A ranger could tag grizzly bears, for example, to learn more about their activities during the fall.

In addition, rangers oversee conservation efforts and might investigate sources of pollution that come from outside the park—such as a factory near a park that is dumping chemicals into a river that travels through the park. Then they would develop plans to help reduce pollution to make the park a better place for plants, animals, and visitors.

Rangers also do bookkeeping and keep other records. They issue permits to visitors and keep track of how many people use the park. In addition, they plan recreational activities and decide how to spend the money budgeted to the park.

Education and Training

Take courses in earth science, biology, mathematics, history, English, and speech. Any classes or activities that deal with plant and animal life, the weather, geography, and interpersonal relationships will be helpful. You should also take courses in government or law to learn about the law enforcement aspects of this career. Since park rangers sometimes work in rugged or demanding physical environments, or have to arrest people who have committed crimes, it is a good idea to take physical education classes.

Park rangers usually have bachelor's degrees in natural resource or recreational resource management. Some rangers

The Most Popular National Parks, 2006

1. **Great Smoky Mountains** (North Carolina, Tennessee)
   http://www.nps.gov/grsm
2. **Grand Canyon** (Arizona)
   http://www.nps.gov/grca
3. **Yosemite** (California)
   http://www.nps.gov/yose
4. **Yellowstone** (Idaho, Montana, Wyoming)
   http://www.nps.gov/yell
5. **Olympic** (Washington)
   http://www.nps.gov/olym
6. **Rocky Mountain** (Colorado)
   http://www.nps.gov/romo
7. **Zion** (Utah)
   http://www.nps.gov/zion
8. **Cuyahoga Valley** (Ohio)
   http://www.nps.gov/cuva
9. **Grand Teton** (Wyoming)
   http://www.nps.gov/grte
10. **Acadia** (Maine)
    http://www.nps.gov/acad

Source: National Park Service (by number of visits)

EXPLORING

○ Read as much as you can about local, state, and national parks. The National Park Service's Web site (http://www.nps.gov) is a great place to start.

○ Get to know your local wildlife. What kind of insects, birds, fish, and other animals live in your area? Your librarian or science teacher will be able to help you find books that identify local flora and fauna.

○ You can gain hands-on experience by getting involved in the Volunteers-in-Parks (VIP) program, which is sponsored by the National Park Service. Volunteers help park employees in many ways, including answering phone calls, welcoming visitors, maintaining trails, building fences, painting buildings, and picking up litter. For more information, visit http://www.nps.gov/volunteer.

○ You also may be able to volunteer at state, county, or local parks. Universities and conservation organizations often have volunteer groups that work on research activities, studies, and rehabilitation efforts.

have degrees in biology or ecology. Classes in forestry, geology, outdoor management, government, history, geography, behavioral sciences, and botany are helpful. Without a degree, you need at least three years of experience working in parks or conservation. Rangers also receive on-the-job training.

Earnings

In 2007, new rangers in the National Park Service earned between $25,623 and $33,309 annually. Rangers with some experience earned between $31,740 and $41,262. The most experienced rangers who supervise other workers earn more than $80,000 a year. The government may provide housing to rangers who work in remote areas.

Rangers in state parks work for the state government. According to the National Association of State Park Directors, rangers employed by state parks had average starting salaries of $24,611 in 2004.

Outlook

The career of park ranger is a popular occupation. The number of people who want to become park rangers is always far greater than the number

To Be a Successful Park Ranger, You Should . . .

○ know about protecting plants and animals

○ be good at explaining the natural environment

○ enjoy working outdoors

○ have a pleasant personality

○ be able to work with different kinds of people

○ be in good physical shape

○ be able to enforce park rules and regulations

of positions available. This trend should continue into the future, and because of the stiff competition for positions, the job outlook for park rangers is expected to change little. As a result, those interested in the field should attain the greatest number and widest variety of applicable skills possible. They

Our National Parks

In 1872, Congress began the U.S. National Park System with the creation of Yellowstone National Park. The National Park Service, a bureau of the U.S. Department of the Interior, was created in 1916 to preserve, protect, and manage the national, cultural, historical, and recreational areas of the National Park System. At that time, the entire park system occupied less than one million acres. Today, the country's national parks cover more than 84 million acres of mountains, plains, deserts, swamps, historic sites, lakeshores, forests, rivers, battlefields, memorials, archaeological properties, and recreation areas.

may wish to study subjects they can also use in other fields, such as forestry, land management, criminal justice, conservation, wildlife management, history, and natural sciences.

FOR MORE INFO

For information about state parks and employment opportunities, contact

National Association of State Park Directors
8829 Woodyhill Road
Raleigh, NC 27613-1134
Tel: 919-676-8365
E-mail: naspd@nc.rr.com
http://www.naspd.org

For general career information, contact the following organization:

National Parks Conservation Association
1300 19th Street NW, Suite 300
Washington, DC 20036-1628
Tel: 800-628-7275
E-mail: npca@npca.org
http://www.npca.org

For detailed information about careers with the National Park Service, contact

National Park Service
U.S. Department of the Interior
1849 C Street NW
Washington, DC 20240-0002
Tel: 202-208-6843
http://www.nps.gov

For information on student volunteer activities and programs, contact

Student Conservation Association
689 River Road
PO Box 550
Charlestown, NH 03603-0550
Tel: 603-543-1700
E-mail: ask-us@sca-inc.org
http://www.thesca.org

Parole Officers

What Parole Officers Do

People who are on parole, called *parolees,* have been released from correctional institutions after serving part of a sentence. *Parole officers* supervise them after their release. Parole officers usually first meet parolees in prison, to explain the conditions of their release.

Parole officers help parolees find a place to live and a new job. They also give advice and emotional support. Sometimes parolees need special help, so an officer may refer them to a counselor or clinic.

Probation officers are similar to parole officers. They supervise offenders who, instead of going to prison, are sentenced to a set amount of time during which they must check in regularly with their officers and follow certain restrictions on their activities.

Parole officers check frequently on parolees to make sure they obey the conditions of their release. Conditions might include attending school or a treatment program, abstaining from drug or alcohol use, and doing community service. Officers keep records for the courts, which include information about parolees' physical and mental health, finances, family, and social activities.

Parole Facts, 2005

- Approximately 784,400 people were on parole in the United States and 4,162,500 were on probation.
- Women made up 12 percent of parolees and 23 percent of probationers.
- Of those paroled 45 percent completed their term of supervision, 38 percent violated the terms of their supervision and were returned to prison, 11 percent did not participate in the parole system and became fugitives.
- States with the largest percentages of their adult populations on parole were Pennsylvania, Arkansas, Oregon, Texas, California, Missouri, South Dakota, Wisconsin, New York, and Illinois.

Source: U.S. Department of Justice

EXPLORING

○ Read books about parole officers and the criminal justice system.

○ There may be a religious or community group in your area that has a program to help rehabilitate parolees. You may try contacting the organization to see if there are volunteer opportunities.

○ Another way to gain exposure to the field is to volunteer for a rehabilitation center or other social service organization. Some agencies offer internship programs for high school and college students interested in the field.

○ Contact a local government agency that handles parole to arrange an information interview with a parole officer.

If a parolee commits further crimes or does not obey the terms of release, a parole officer begins procedures to return the parolee to a correctional institution. Officers in some states arrest troublesome parolees. Working with parolees is sometimes dangerous.

Education and Training

To prepare for a career as a parole officer, take English, social science, civics, government, and psychology classes. Learning a foreign language will also be helpful.

Parole officers must have a bachelor's degree in criminal justice, social work, psychology, law, or a related field. Government agencies require a master's degree and experience in social work.

Earnings

The U.S. Department of Labor reports that the median annual earnings for probation officers and correctional treatment specialists (the category under which parole officers are classified) were $42,500 in 2006. Salaries ranged from less than $28,000 to $71,160 or more. Parole officers employed in state government earned a mean salary of $47,570 in 2006. Those employed in local government earned $45,380. Educational level also affects salary. Parole officers with advanced degrees generally earn more than those with bachelor's degrees.

The Parole System Begins

A system of conditional and early release did not begin in the United States until the 1870s in New York. By 1916, every state and the District of Columbia had established a similar program. This system of early release from prison came to be called *parole*—French for word—because prisoners were freed on their word, or parole, of honor.

Outlook

The employment outlook for parole officers is good, according to the U.S. Department of Labor. The number of prisoners increased dramatically during the past decade and many of these will become eligible for parole. The overcrowding of prisons, combined with the high cost of keeping someone in jail, will lead to the early release of many convicts who will require supervision. However, public outcry over leniency toward convicted criminals, particularly repeat offenders, has created demand and even legislation for stiffer penalties and the withdrawal of the possibility of parole for many crimes. This development may ultimately decrease the demand for parole officers, as more and more criminals serve their full sentences.

FOR MORE INFO

Contact the ACA for information on careers.
American Correctional Association (ACA)
206 North Washington Street, Suite 200
Alexandria, VA 22314-2528
Tel: 703-224-0000
http://www.aca.org

For information on probation and parole, contact
American Probation and Parole Association
2760 Research Park Drive
Lexington, KY 40511-8410
Tel: 859-244-8203
http://www.appa-net.org

Police Officers

What Police Officers Do

Police officers protect people and their property by upholding and enforcing laws. They keep the peace, prevent criminal acts, and arrest people who break the law.

Some officers patrol public places, such as parks or streets, to make sure no one breaks the law. These laws tell people not to speed, drink alcoholic beverages in public places, fight, or otherwise cause disorder. Police officers patrol on foot, in squad cars, on motorcycles, on bicycles, or on horseback. They also search for missing children, stolen cars or other property, and persons wanted by law enforcement agencies.

Some police officers direct traffic during busy times of the day and ticket motorists who break traffic laws (such as those that restrict speeding, improper lane usage, or loud music). Others protect government buildings, including courthouses.

Police officers also help people during emergencies. They provide first aid to accident victims, see that sick or injured

Words to Learn

probable cause information uncovered by officers that gives them a reason to arrest, search, or stop and detain a person

reasonable suspicion the reasons an officer believes a person should be stopped and detained

surveillance following, observing, or listening to people for the purpose of obtaining information about criminal activities

people are rushed to hospitals, and help firefighters by controlling crowds and rerouting traffic. Police officers also prevent or break up violent disturbances.

Most police officers are trained to use firearms and carry guns. Police in special divisions, such as chemical analysis and handwriting and fingerprint identification, have special training. Officers often testify in court regarding the cases they handle. Police also have to complete accurate and thorough records of their cases.

Education and Training

It is difficult to become a police officer. You must pass many tests to prove you are qualified. These tests include written exams and tests of physical strength, endurance, and dexterity. You will be checked to see if you have any medical condition (such as a heart problem) that might hinder your work. There are background checks to make sure you are a U.S. citizen and have no history of criminal activity or convictions.

Today, most police departments require that applicants have a high school diploma. Many departments in larger cities require some college training. Many four-year and junior colleges now offer programs in law enforcement, police work, and police administration.

New police recruits receive special training. This may last from three to six months or longer. Training usually includes classroom work in local, state, and federal laws; firearm

EXPLORING

○ Play games and make up exercises to test your memory and powers of observation. For example, you might play a DVD you have never seen before. Advance to a random spot and play it for 30 seconds. Stop the disk and write down everything you observed. Describe the setting, the people, their clothing, the conversation, the background noise, and anything else you observed. Then replay the clip and check your accuracy. Try this with friends and compare notes.

○ Many police departments have programs for kids. Look for educational events that teach you about street safety, Internet safety, or self-defense.

○ Participate in police-sponsored sports events or social activities. It will give you a chance to meet and talk with police officers.

A police officer picks up a shell casing at the scene of a shooting. (Mike Greenlar, Syracuse Newspapers, The Image Works)

instruction; physical fitness training; and legal procedures for enforcing the law.

Earnings

According to the U.S. Department of Labor, police officers earned an annual average salary of $47,460 in 2006. Salaries ranged from less than $27,310 to $72,450 or more annually. Police officers in supervisory positions earned median salaries of $69,310 a year in 2006, with a low of less than $41,260 and a high of more than $104,410.

Salaries for police officers range widely based on location. Police departments in the West and North generally pay more than those in the South.

It's a Fact

Sir Robert Peel established the first modern, nonmilitary police force in 1829 in London, England. The British police became known as bobbies after Sir Robert's name. The police force in New York City was established in 1844. These new police officers wore uniforms, worked 24 hours a day, and often carried guns as they patrolled the streets. On the American frontier, laws were often enforced by volunteer police officers. Many areas of the West were guarded by a sheriff and the sheriff's deputies. An effort to establish a statewide police force resulted in the creation of the Texas Rangers in 1835. In 1905, Pennsylvania formed the first official state police department. Soon, almost every state had a state police department as well as police units that worked for individual cities or towns.

Outlook

Employment of police officers is expected to grow about as fast as the average, according to the U.S. Department of Labor. Despite this prediction, there is a lot of competition for jobs. This occupation has a very low turnover rate. However, jobs should become available as officers move into higher positions, retire, or leave the force for other reasons. Police officers retire early compared to people in other careers. Many retire while in their 40s or 50s and then pursue second careers.

In the past 10 years, private security firms have taken over some police activities, such as patrolling airports and other public places. Some private companies even provide police forces for entire cities. Many companies and universities also operate their own police forces.

FOR MORE INFO

For information on careers in policing, contact
International Police Association
http://www.ipa-usa.org

The National Association of Police Organizations is a coalition of police unions and associations that work to advance the interests of law enforcement officers through legislation, political action, and education.
National Association of Police Organizations
317 South Patrick Street
Alexandria, VA 22314-3501
Tel: 703-549-0775
E-mail: info@napo.org
http://www.napo.org

Polygraph Examiners

What Polygraph Examiners Do

Polygraph examiners give and evaluate polygraph, or lie detector, tests. During a polygraph examination, an examiner asks the test subject certain questions. As the individual answers yes or no, any changes in his or her breathing rate, blood pressure, heartbeat, and skin condition are measured by the polygraph device. After the test, the examiner studies the results and compares them with responses to questions whose answers are known to be true. By carefully comparing the responses, the examiner judges whether or not the test questions have been answered truthfully.

A polygraph examiner tests a subject. (Bob Daemmrich, The Image Works)

Polygraph examiners work for local, state, or federal courts to help determine whether individuals accused of crimes are telling the truth. They also work for the FBI, for the U.S. Secret Service, and for police and sheriff departments. Some examiners have their own agencies, and others teach in lie-detection schools.

To work as a polygraph examiner, you must show good moral character and must not have a police record. You should speak and write well, have self-confidence, be alert, and be able to maintain objectivity and self-control.

You also must be comfortable working with strangers and relate well to all kinds of people. It is crucial to show fairness; you should not be influenced by factors such as economic status, race, or sex.

In addition, you must be willing to work under pressure and under a variety of conditions and should not be shocked by distressing sights. You must understand the importance of protecting your subjects' rights and maintaining confidentiality.

Education and Training

You should take courses in high school that help you understand how the body functions and how it is affected by stress. Courses in psychology, physiology, and biology will be especially useful. In general, take courses that will prepare you for college.

A college major in science or criminal justice will prepare you for this career. In addition, classes in English and writing will help prepare you to write reports, and classes in public speaking will help you develop the self-confidence you will need when testifying in court.

EXPLORING

○ Read books and magazines about polygraph equipment and techniques.
○ Visit the American Polygraph Association's Web site (http://www.polygraph.org/glossary.cfm) for a glossary of terms and more information on the field.
○ If you are interested in a career in this field, you may be able to visit lie-detection schools and talk with staff members. You also may be able to visit courts and tour police facilities.
○ Because polygraph examiners must obtain cooperation from their test subjects, activities that offer contact with people can provide you valuable experience. Such activities include summer work as a camp counselor and volunteer or part-time work in a hospital or nursing home.

Candidates for lie-detection schools usually need four-year college degrees, but applicants with two years of college courses in criminal investigation plus five years of investigative experience may be accepted. Polygraph training in an approved school usually takes six to eight weeks.

The Employee Polygraph Protection Act

Lie-detector testing has sparked a great deal of controversy. Many people object to such testing as an invasion of privacy and a violation of civil liberties. The validity of polygraph tests has often been questioned, and test results are generally inadmissible in court unless the defense, prosecution, and judge agree to their use. While studies have rated the validity of polygraph examinations at 80 to 98 percent, their reliability depends on the skill and experience of the examiner.

This controversy resulted in federal legislation. In 1988, the federal government established the Employee Polygraph Protection Act, which placed strict controls on the use of polygraph testing by private employers. Businesses are prohibited from requiring polygraph testing of employees or job applicants, except for employers engaged in security services, toxic waste disposal, or controlled substances, and employers under contract with the federal government. Polygraph testing is also permitted when an individual is suspected of committing a finance-related crime.

You must take polygraph tests upon entering a lie-detection school to ensure that you have the good moral character this field requires. During your training, you learn to operate the polygraph, develop and ask questions, interpret test results, understand the legal aspects of polygraph testing, and read the physical responses the polygraph measures. You observe polygraph tests administered by others, administer the tests yourself, and hear and see audiotapes and videotapes of your own performances.

After you complete your study in lie detection, you go on to an internship of at least six months before becoming fully qualified as a polygraph examiner. Although many states license polygraph examiners, requirements vary.

Earnings

Polygraph examiners beginning their internships may earn from $18,000 to $30,000 a year, and experienced examiners earn as much as $60,000 a year or more.

The salaries of polygraph examiners are comparable to those of other law enforcement investigators. According to the U.S. Department of Labor, median annual earnings of private detectives and investigators were $33,750 in 2006, ranging from less than $19,720 to more than $64,380. Median annual earnings of detectives and criminal investigators were $58,260, with salaries ranging from less than $34,480 to more than $92,590.

Outlook

Because of recent restrictions, there are fewer positions for private polygraph examiners than a decade ago. However, there is an increasing need for law enforcement examiners, especially in the federal government.

The growing population and increasing crime rate may create more openings for polygraph examiners in the future. Courts in at least 30 states allow the use of polygraph test results as evidence. Public pressure to reduce court backlogs may increase the use of polygraph tests.

FOR MORE INFO

For a list of polygraph schools, contact
American Association of Police Polygraphists
PO Box 657
Waynesville, OH 45068-0657
Tel: 888-743-5479
http://www.wordnet.net/aapp

For general information about polygraph testing, as well as information on licensing and accredited polygraph schools and training, contact
American Polygraph Association
PO Box 8037
Chattanooga, TN 37414-0037
Tel: 800-272-8037
http://www.polygraph.org

Process Servers

What Process Servers Do

Process servers are licensed by the courts to serve legal papers, such as summonses (an order to appear before the court), subpoenas (a formal request that asks a person to come to court to testify), and court orders, to people involved in legal disputes. People served may include witnesses, defendants in lawsuits, or the employers of workers whose wages are being garnished (an order of the court that calls for the served person to bring certain property before the court).

Process servers are responsible for notifying people in a timely and legal fashion that they are required to appear in court. They work for attorneys, government agencies (such as a state's attorney general's office), or any person who files a lawsuit, seeks a divorce, or begins a legal action.

A process server is involved only in civil matters. Criminal arrest warrants or papers ordering the seizure of property are served exclusively by sheriffs, constables, and other law enforcement officials. To ensure that private process servers aren't mistaken for law enforcement officials, most jurisdictions forbid process servers to wear uniforms and badges or to place official-looking emblems on their vehicles.

Process servers know the rules of civil procedure, such as expiration dates

How to Find Someone

Some people try to avoid being served by a process server. Here are a few of the methods process servers use to track down these individuals:

○ searching public records on the Internet

○ talking to neighbors and coworkers

○ checking with government agencies for public information on the individual

○ conducting surveillance of places the individual often visits

of court documents. Subpoenas, eviction notices (an order that forces an individual to leave his or her home or another setting), notices of trustee sales (an order that property or goods owned by an individual must be sold because he or she has not paid for them), writs of garnishment, summonses, and court orders each must be served according to complicated regulations. The process server is responsible for making sure that every service is valid by following these rules and exceptions.

Much of a process server's time is spent skip-tracing—that is, trying to locate a person who has moved or who may be avoiding service. Process servers sometimes have to search for a last-known address, a place of business, or even a photograph of the person. They question neighbors or coworkers and use public information provided by government offices (such as the assessor's office), voter registration, or the court clerk to locate the person. They also use the Internet to conduct research.

EXPLORING

○ Visit the Web sites of professional associations (see "For More Info") to learn more about the career.

○ Since most court records are public, you could look at actual files of court cases to familiarize yourself with the types of papers served and to examine affidavits (a written statement made under oath to an officer of the court) filed by process servers. Ask your parent or guardian to help you do this.

○ Contact process servers and ask for information about the field. Both the National Association of Professional Process Servers and the United States Process Servers Association provide lists of process servers at their Web sites.

The actual service of the paper is a simple process. The process server identifies himself or herself as an officer of the court, tells the person that he or she is being served, and hands the person the documents. If the person won't accept service, or won't confirm his or her identity, the process server drops papers or simply leaves the documents. In the eyes of the court, the person is considered served whether or not he or she actually touches the papers, signs for them, or even acknowledges the process server's presence.

To Be a Successful Process Server, You Should . . .

○ be bold, confident, and skilled at working with people

○ have good organizational skills

○ be reliable and responsible

○ be willing to travel

○ be comfortable with a certain amount of danger

Education and Training

To prepare for a career as a process server, take courses in English, political science, communications, and any law or business-related subjects. Training in a foreign language can also be extremely helpful because process servers may encounter non-English speakers.

Although college is not required, advanced courses in psychology, communications, business, and legal studies are beneficial to process servers. Organizations, such as the Process Server Institute (see "For More Info"), hold training seminars that focus directly on process serving.

Earnings

Earnings for process servers vary according to the number and type of papers served. A salaried employee who works part time as a process server can expect to make approximately $27,000, although a salaried, full-time process server can expect almost twice as much, approximately $45,000 to $50,000.

Outlook

Employment opportunities for process servers will grow as the number of civil lawsuits increases. A single legal case can produce anywhere from one service to dozens, when taking into account subpoenas, supporting orders, writs of garnishment, and other documents.

Some sheriff's departments are now beginning to rely solely on private process servers, since they cannot effectively compete with the faster and more inexpensive private process-serving companies. Other jurisdictions, increasingly under pressure to justify serving civil papers at a loss, are likely to revise their laws as well.

FOR MORE INFO

For information on professional resources and training, contact
National Association of Professional Process Servers
PO Box 4547
Portland, OR 97208-4547
Tel: 800-477-8211
E-mail: administrator@napps.org
http://www.napps.com

Process Server Institute
667 Folsom Street, 2nd Floor
San Francisco, CA 94107-1314
Tel: 415-495-3850
E-mail: psinstitute@juno.com
http://www.psinstitute.com

For a listing of current process servers, contact
United States Process Servers Association
PO Box 19767
St. Louis, MO 63144-0167
Tel: 866-367-2841
http://www.usprocessservers.com

Secret Service Special Agents

What Secret Service Special Agents Do

Secret Service special agents are employed by the U.S. Secret Service, which is part of the Department of Homeland Security. They work to protect the president and other political leaders of the United States, as well as heads of foreign states or governments when they are visiting the United States. Special agents also investigate financial crimes, such as the counterfeiting of U.S. currency. Special agents can carry and use firearms, execute warrants, and make arrests.

An individual who is guarded by the Secret Service is known as a protectee. For example, if the president plans to make a speech at a convention center, an advance team of special agents visits the location ahead of time. These agents

Words to Learn

choke point a potential ambush site—like a bridge—where a protectee or motorcade may be more vulnerable to attack

protectee a person—usually a U.S. politician or a foreign dignitary—who the Secret Service is responsible for protecting; protectees may also include the spouse or family of the primary protectee

protective bubble a 360-degree boundary of safety that the Secret Service maintains around each of its protectees; special agents try to prevent dangers from penetrating the bubble

identify hospitals, exit routes, and potential choke points, and they work closely with local police, fire, and rescue units to develop a protection plan. They set up a command post as the communication center for protective activities. Before the president arrives, a *lead advance agent* works with members of all the other law enforcement agencies that are assisting with the visit. He or she tells agents where they will be posted and notifies them about any special concerns. Agents set up checkpoints and limit access to the secure area just before the president arrives. During the president's speech, they establish a protective bubble, monitor the area, and observe people in the crowd to make sure that no one attempts to hurt the president.

EXPLORING

○ Visit the Student Q&A page on the Secret Service Web site (http://www.secretservice.gov/kids_faq.shtml).

○ The Secret Service offers the Stay-In-School Program for high school students. The program allows students who meet financial eligibility guidelines to earn money by working for the agency part time, usually in a clerical job. Contact the Secret Service for more information.

After the visit, special agents study every step of the operation, record unusual incidents, and suggest improvements for the future.

When Secret Service special agents are not protecting the president or other officials, they conduct criminal investigations. For example, they investigate threats made to protectees. They also investigate cases of counterfeit currency and financial crimes that include financial institution fraud, identity theft, computer fraud, and computer-based attacks on our nation's banking, financial, and telecommunications systems.

Education and Training

In high school, take computer science, foreign language, government, English, and physical education classes to prepare for this career.

Secret Service Special Agents guard the president's limousine during the inaugural parade in Washington, D.C., in 2005. (Rick Wilking, Reuters, Corbis)

Once you graduate from high school, there are several ways to qualify for entry into the Secret Service. Some people earn a bachelor's degree. Others work for at least three years in a criminal investigative or law enforcement field and then enter the Secret Service.

All newly hired agents participate in 9 weeks of training at the Federal Law Enforcement Training Center in Glynco, Georgia. This is followed by 11 weeks of specialized training at the Secret Service's Training Academy in Beltsville, Maryland.

Special agents must be U.S. citizens; be at least 21 at the time of appointment; pass a vision test; pass an examination; and undergo a complete background investigation.

Earnings

Agents usually start at the GS-5, GS-7, or GS-9 grade levels (pay scales established by the federal government), which were $25,623, $31,740, and $38,824 in 2007, respectively. Agents who live in areas that have a higher cost of living may earn slightly higher salaries. Agents automatically advance by two pay grades each year, until they reach the GS-12 level, which was $56,301 in 2007. Agents must compete for positions above

Then and Now

It is the Secret Service's responsibility to protect the following people:

○ the president and vice president (also president-elect and vice president–elect) and their immediate families

○ former presidents and their spouses for 10 years after the president leaves office

○ children of former presidents until they are 16 years old

○ visiting heads of foreign states or governments and their spouses

○ official representatives of the United States who are performing special missions abroad

○ major presidential and vice-presidential candidates and, within 120 days of the general presidential election, their spouses

○ other individuals as designated per Executive Order of the president and National Special Security Events, when designated as such by the secretary of the Department of Homeland Security

the GS-12 level; however, the majority of agents become a GS-13—$66,951 in 2007—in their career.

Outlook

The Secret Service is a small federal law enforcement agency. It employs about 6,400 people, 3,200 of whom are special agents. As a result, the number of agents it hires each year is low. Individuals with advanced education and previous experience in law enforcement will have the best chance of becoming a special agent.

FOR MORE INFO

Your local Secret Service field office can provide more information on becoming a special agent. If you contact the headquarters and are writing about the Stay-In-School program, mark the envelope "Attention: Stay-In-School Program."

U.S. Secret Service
245 Murray Drive, Building 410
Washington, DC 20223-0004
Tel: 202-406-5708
http://www.secretservice.gov

Security Consultants and Guards

What Security Consultants and Guards Do

Security guards keep public and private property safe from theft, vandalism, fire, and illegal entry. Sports arenas, office buildings, banks, schools, hospitals, and stores are a few of the places that security guards protect. For example, a *bank guard* monitors an area to ensure that money is not stolen from a bank, and an *office guard* will stop certain people from entering the building.

Other names for the various kinds of security guards are *patroller, bouncer, gate tender, armored-car guard,* and *airline security representative.*

Most security guards wear some type of uniform. However, in situations where it is important for guards to blend in with the general public, they wear ordinary clothes. They might be assigned to one spot, such as at an entry to a building, where they answer people's questions, give directions, or keep possible troublemakers away. Other guards make rounds, or regular tours, of a building or its surrounding land to make sure the property is safe and secure.

Security guards may sign visitors in and out of a building in order to keep track of who is in the building at any given time, direct traffic at a concert or some other type of crowded event, enforce no-smoking rules, or inspect people's packages as they come into a building. They often carry two-way radios so they can communicate with other guards. Those who are likely to encounter criminal activity in their work may also carry guns.

Security consultants do protective service work of a different nature. They develop security plans as a means of protection, and they are involved in preventing theft, vandalism, fraud, kidnapping, and other crimes.

Security consultants often work with companies to help them protect their equipment and records from unwanted intruders. They study the physical conditions of a facility, observe how a company conducts its operations, and then discuss options with company officials. For example, a large company that produces military equipment may be advised to fence its property and place electronic surveillance equipment at several points along the fence. The company may also be advised to install closed-circuit television cameras and to hire several security guards to monitor restricted areas. A smaller company may need only to install burglar alarms around specially restricted areas. Consultants analyze all the possibilities and then present a written proposal to management for approval.

EXPLORING

○ Read books and magazines about security issues and professionals in the field.
○ Join a safety patrol at school. Volunteer to serve as a crossing guard, hall monitor, or fire monitor.
○ Ask your guidance counselor to help arrange an information interview with a security guard or consultant. Ask the following questions: Can you describe a typical day on the job? What do you like least and most about your job? How did you train for this field? What advice would you give a young person who is interested in the field?

Education and Training

Most employers prefer to hire guards who have at least a high school education. A security guard should be healthy, alert, calm in emergencies, and able to follow directions. Good eyesight and hearing are important, too. People who have had military or police experience are often considered to be good candidates for security guard jobs. Some employers may ask applicants to take vision, hearing, or aptitude tests. For some security guard jobs, experience with firearms is required. Applicants for certain guard positions may have to pass a security check, assuring that they have never been guilty of a serious crime.

Security consultants need a college degree. An undergraduate or associate's degree in criminal justice, business administration, or related field is best.

Earnings

Earnings for security consultants vary greatly depending on the consultant's training and experience. Entry-level consultants with bachelor's degrees commonly start at $26,000 to $32,000 per year. Consultants with graduate degrees begin at $34,000 to $41,000 per year. Experienced consultants may earn $50,000 to $100,000 per year or more.

Average starting salaries for security guards and technicians vary according to their level of training and experience, and the location where they work. Median annual earnings for security guards were $21,530 in 2006, according to the U.S. Department of Labor. Experienced security guards earned more than

---

To Be a Successful Security Guard, You Should . . .

○ be in good general health

○ have good vision and hearing

○ be emotionally stable

○ have integrity

○ have strong communication skills

○ be able to follow directions

○ have a clean police record

$35,840 per year in 2006. The least experienced security guards earned less than $15,030 annually.

Outlook

Employment for guards and other security personnel is expected to grow as fast as the average, as crime rates rise with the overall population growth. Public concern about crime and terrorism continues to increase. Many job openings will be created as a result of the high turnover of workers in this field.

Another factor adding to the demand for security professionals is the trend for private security firms to perform duties previously handled by police officers, such as courtroom security. Private security companies employ security technicians to guard many government sites, such as nuclear testing facilities; operate many training facilities for government security technicians and guards; and provide police services for some communities.

FOR MORE INFO

For information on educational programs, contact
ASIS International
1625 Prince Street
Alexandria, VA 22314-2818
Tel: 703-519-6200
E-mail: asis@asisonline.org
http://www.asisonline.org

For information on union membership, contact the SPFPA.
Security, Police, and Fire Professionals of America (SPFPA)
http://www.spfpa.org

Glossary

accredited approved as meeting established standards for providing good training and education; this approval is usually given by an independent organization of professionals

apprentice a person who is learning a trade by working under the supervision of a skilled worker; apprentices often receive classroom instruction in addition to their supervised practical experience

associate's degree an academic rank or title granted by a community or junior college or similar institution to graduates of a two-year program of education beyond high school

bachelor's degree an academic rank or title given to a person who has completed a four-year program of study at a college or university; also called an undergraduate degree or baccalaureate

career an occupation for which a worker receives training and has an opportunity for advancement

certified approved as meeting established requirements for skill, knowledge, and experience in a particular field; people are certified by the organization of professionals in their field

college a higher education institution that is above the high school level

community college a public or private two-year college attended by students who do not usually live at the college; graduates of a community college receive an associate's degree and may transfer to a four-year college or university to complete a bachelor's degree

diploma   a certificate or document given by a school to show that a person has completed a course or has graduated from the school

distance education   a type of educational program that allows students to take classes and complete their education by mail or the Internet

doctorate   the highest academic rank or title granted by a graduate school to a person who has completed a two- to three-year program after having received a master's degree

fringe benefit   a payment or benefit to an employee in addition to regular wages or salary; examples of fringe benefits include a pension, paid vacation time, and health or life insurance

graduate school   a school that people may attend after they have received their bachelor's degree; people who complete an educational program at a graduate school earn a master's degree or a doctorate

intern   an advanced student (usually one with at least some college training) in a professional field who is employed in a job that is intended to provide supervised practical experience for the student

internship   (1) The position or job of an intern; (2) the period of time when a person is an intern

junior college   a two-year college that offers courses like those in the first half of a four-year college program; graduates of a junior college usually receive an associate's degree and may transfer to a four-year college or university to complete a bachelor's degree

liberal arts   the subjects covered by college courses that develop broad general knowledge rather than specific occupational skills; the liberal arts often include philosophy, literature and the arts, history, language, and some courses in the social sciences and natural sciences

licensed   having formal permission from the proper authority to carry out an activity that would be illegal without that permission;

for example, a person must be licensed to practice medicine or drive a car

major the academic field in which a college student specializes and receives a degree

master's degree an academic rank or title granted by a graduate school to a person who has completed a one- or two-year program after having received a bachelor's degree

pension an amount of money paid regularly by an employer to a former employee after he or she retires from working

scholarship a gift of money to a student to help the student pay for further education

social studies courses of study (such as civics, geography, and history) that deal with how human societies work

starting salary salary paid to a newly hired employee; the starting salary is usually a smaller amount than is paid to a more experienced worker

technical college a private or public college offering two- or four-year programs in technical subjects; technical colleges offer courses in both general and technical subjects and award associate's and bachelor's degrees

technician a worker with specialized practical training in a mechanical or scientific subject who works under the supervision of scientists, engineers, or other professionals; technicians typically receive two years of college-level education after high school

technologist a worker in a mechanical or scientific field with more training than a technician; technologists typically must have between two and four years of college-level education after high school

undergraduate a student at a college or university who has not yet received a degree

undergraduate degree see bachelor's degree

union an organization whose members are workers in a particular industry or company; the union works to gain better wages, benefits, and working conditions for its members; also called a labor union or trade union

vocational school a public or private school that offers training in one or more skills or trades

wage money that is paid in return for work done, especially money paid on the basis of the number of hours or days worked

Index of Job Titles

A

administrative analysts 21
agricultural inspectors 53
airline security
  representatives 80
air marshals 5
airport security workers
  5–8
armored-car guards 80

B

baggage and passenger
  screeners 5
bank guards 80
border patrol agents 9–12
bouncers 80
bounty hunters 13–16

C

canine enforcement officers
  27
CBP agriculture specialists
  24–25
corrections officers 17–19
crime analysts 20–23
criminal investigators 27
criminalists 48–51
customers officials 24–27
Customs and Border
  Protection chemists 27
Customs and Border
  Protection (CBP) officers
  24–26, 53
customs pilots 27

D

deputy U.S. marshals 28–31
detectives 32–35

E

environmental health
  inspectors 53

F

FBI agents 36–39
fingerprint classifiers 49
firefighters 44–47
fire inspectors and
  investigators 40–45
fire marshals 41
food and drug inspectors 53
forensic anthropologists 49
forensic experts 48–51
forensic odontologists 49
forensic pathologists 49
forensic psychiatrists 49
forensic toxicologists 49

G

gate tenders 80
geneticists 49

H

health and regulatory
  inspectors 52–55

I

identification technicians 49
import specialists 27

L
lead advance agents 77

M
molecular biologists 49

O
occupational safety and
  health inspectors 53
office guards 80

P
park rangers 56–60
parole officers 61–63
patrollers 80
police officers 64–67
polygraph examiners 68–71

private investigators 32–35
probation officers 61
process servers 72–75

S
secret service special agents
  76–79
security agents 5
security consultants and
  guards 80–83
security directors 5
security screeners 5
special agents 27
strategic analysts 21

T
tactical analysts 21

Browse and Learn More

Books

Ackerman, Thomas H. *FBI Careers: The Ultimate Guide to Landing a Job as One of America's Finest.* 2d ed. Indianapolis, Ind.: JIST Works, 2005.

Bishop, Matt. *Introduction to Computer Security.* Upper Saddle River, N.J.: Addison-Wesley Professional, 2004.

Bowers, Vivien. *Crime Scene: How Investigators Use Science to Track Down the Bad Guys.* 2d ed. Toronto, Canada: Maple Tree Press, 2006.

Broyles, Matthew. *U.S. Air Marshals.* New York: Rosen Publishing Group, 2007.

Bullock, Jane A., et al. *Introduction to Homeland Security.* 2d ed. Burlington, Mass.: Butterworth-Heinemann, 2006.

Cefrey, Holly. *Bounty Hunter.* New York: Children's Press, 2003.

Croce, Nicholas. *Detectives: Life Investigating Crime.* Rosen Publishing Group, 2003.

Davenport, John C. *Global Extremism and Terrorism.* New York: Chelsea House Publications, 2007.

De Capua, Sarah. *The FBI.* New York: Children's Press, 2007.

Fridell, Ron. *Forensic Science.* Minneapolis, Minn.: Lerner Publications, 2006.

Gaines, Ann. *Border Patrol Agent and Careers in Border Protection.* Berkeley Heights, N.J.: Enslow Publishers, 2006.

———. *Special Agent and Careers in the FBI.* Berkeley Heights, N.J.: Enslow Publishers, 2006.

Harry, J. Scott, and Karen M. Hess. *Careers in Criminal Justice and Related Fields: From Internship to Promotion.* 5th ed. Belmont, Calif.: Thomson/Wadsworth, 2005.

Hopping, Lorraine. *Bone Detective: The Story of Forensic Anthropologist Diane France.* Washington, D.C.: Joseph Henry Press, 2006.

Parks, Peggy. *Exploring Careers: Firefighter.* Farmington Hills, Mich.: KidHaven Press, 2004.

———. *Exploring Careers: Police Officer.* Farmington Hills, Mich.: KidHaven Press, 2003.

Peterson's. *Peterson's Summer Opportunities for Kids & Teenagers.* 24th ed. Lawrenceville, N.J.: Peterson's, 2006.

Souter, Gerry. *Secret Service Agent and Careers in Federal Protection.* Berkeley Heights, N.J.: Enslow Publishers, 2006.

Souter, Janet. *Air Marshal and Careers in Transportation Security.* Berkeley Heights, N.J.: Enslow Publishers, 2007.

Thomas, William David. *Working in Law Enforcement.* Strongsville, Ohio: Gareth Stevens Publishing, 2005.

Tyska, Louis A., and Lawrence J. Fennelly. *Investigations: 150 Things You Should Know.* New York: Butterworth-Heineman, 1999.

Wagner, E. J. *The Science of Sherlock Holmes: From Baskerville Hall to the Valley of Fear, the Real Forensics Behind the Great Detective's Greatest Cases.* Hoboken, N.J.: Wiley, 2007.

Wiese, Jim. *Detective Science: 40 Crime-Solving, Case-Breaking, Crook-Catching Activities for Kids.* San Francisco: Jossey-Bass, 1996.

Web Sites

American Library Association: Great Web Sites for Kids
http://www.ala.org/greatsites

Central Intelligence Agency: Kids Page
https://www.cia.gov/kids-page/index.html

Consumer Product Safety Commission: Kidd Safety
http://www.cpsc.gov/kids/kidsafety

Drug Enforcement Administration: Get It Straight
http://www.usdoj.gov/dea/pubs/straight/cover.htm

Federal Bureau of Investigation: Kids' Page
http://www.fbi.gov/fbikids.htm

FireSafety.gov for Kids

http://www.firesafety.gov/kids/flash.shtm

Maryland Department of State Police for Kids

http://www.mdsp.org/kids/default.asp

McGruff.org (Sponsored by the National Crime Prevention Council)

http://www.mcgruff.org

National Fire Protection Association

http://www.nfpa.org

U.S. Environmental Protection Agency: Environmental Kids Club

http://www.epa.gov/kids

U.S. Fire Administration for Kids

http://www.usfa.dhs.gov/kids/flash.shtm

U.S. Food and Drug Administration: Kids' Home Page

http://www.fda.gov/oc/opacom/kids/default.htm

U.S. Marshals for Students of All Ages

http://www.usmarshals.gov/usmsforkids